STICKLEY
CRAFTSMAN FURNITURE
CATALOGS

Unabridged Reprints of
Two Mission Furniture Catalogs

"Craftsman Furniture Made by Gustav Stickley"

and

"The Work of L. & J.G. Stickley"

With a new introduction by
DAVID M. CATHERS

DOVER PUBLICATIONS, INC., NEW YORK

Published in Canada by General Publishing Company, Ltd.,
30 Lesmill Road, Don Mills, Toronto, Ontario.
Published in the United Kingdom by Constable and Company, Ltd.

This Dover edition, first published in 1979, is an unabridged
republication of the following two booklets:
(1) *Catalogue of Craftsman Furniture Made by Gustav
Stickley at The Craftsman Workshops[,] Eastwood, N.Y.*, published by Gustav Stickley in 1910.
(2) *The Work of L. & J. G. Stickley[,] Fayetteville, New York*,
n.d.
This edition also contains a new introduction by David M.
Cathers.
The publisher is grateful to Mr. Scott Elliott of Helios
Gallery in New York for calling his attention to these works
and for making copies of the originals available for reproduction.

International Standard Book Number: 0-486-23838-5
Library of Congress Catalog Card Number: 79-50653

Manufactured in the United States of America
Dover Publications, Inc.
180 Varick Street
New York, N.Y. 10014

INTRODUCTION TO THE
DOVER EDITION

GUSTAV STICKLEY

The September 1910 issue of Gustav Stickley's magazine *The Craftsman* proudly announced that his new catalog was "just off the press." That catalog is reproduced in the first part of the present volume.

Stickley's catalogs were clearly important to him. He apparently produced one every year between 1901 and 1913, although as of this writing catalogs for 1903, 1908 and 1911 are not known. His catalogs enabled him to sell his Craftsman furniture directly to the consumer; from 1901 through 1904 he attempted to bypass the furniture trade and relied heavily upon his catalogs, *The Craftsman* and his showrooms at the Craftsman Building in Syracuse, New York to sell his products. Craftsman furniture was available through very few retailers during those years. By 1904 he was seeking a wider market and began to establish a national network of "associates," furniture dealers across the country who sold his products. Yet he continued to announce his new catalogs in *The Craftsman* and to encourage his readers to send for them.

However, Stickley's catalogs were never solely intended as a means to promote sales. They were also conveyors of his Arts and Crafts philosophy, teaching devices through which he preached his gospel of sturdiness and simplicity. Seen in this light, his catalogs are more than interesting documents of early twentieth-century American applied arts; they are also embodiments of social history.

The earliest known advertisement for Stickley's furniture was headlined "Furniture As An Educator." Throughout his career, he believed that furniture, indeed the entire home environment, exerted a strong moral influence on the inhabitants. Consequently, well-made, well-designed furniture was not simply a practical or esthetic necessity, it was also a moral imperative. Stickley expressed this belief very clearly in his introduction to the present catalog: "I felt that badly constructed, over-ornate, meaningless furniture . . . was not only bad in itself, but that its presence in the homes of people was an influence that led directly away from the sound qualities which make an honest man and a good citizen."

There is no reason to doubt the sincerity of Stickley's words. Although he was a furniture maker, a manufacturer trying to sell his products and make a profit, he was also a man of high ideals. In *The Craftsman* he published plans showing exactly how to make Craftsman furniture, and most of the designs were taken from his own work. In this 1910 catalog, in the brief section on metalwork (page 82), he wrote: "We also supply amateur cabinetmakers with the same metal trim which we use ourselves so that when they make Craftsman furniture in their own workshops from designs which we furnish them, they need not be at a loss for the right metal trim." In the fabric and needlework section (page 97), he said: "To those of our patrons who like to do such needlework at home we send on request prices of materials stamped with any design selected and sufficient floss for working." Stickley was perfectly willing to give home craftsworkers the opportunity to duplicate the very goods he was selling. He believed in the Arts and Crafts virtues of

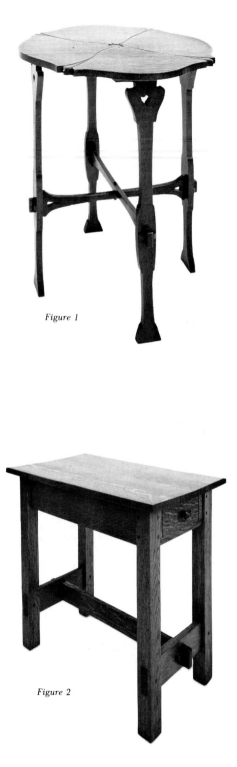

Figure 1

Figure 2

self-sufficiency and joy in work, and he practiced what he preached—even if it meant reduced sales of his own Craftsman goods.

However, it is Stickley's furniture more than his philosophy that interests us here. The 1910 catalog is in many ways a pivotal one, for it signals the beginnings of a shift in his work. Perhaps the best way to understand this point is to examine the development of his Craftsman style from its very beginning.

Until 1898, Stickley had been a fairly typical late nineteenth-century furniture manufacturer. Throughout the 1880s and into the early 1890s he and his four brothers produced and sold "walnut parlor suits" and other ordinary late Victorian furniture. In the mid-1890s he and a partner, Elgin Simonds, were manufacturing reproduction Chippendale pieces in Syracuse, New York. But as the 1890s drew to a close, Stickley came increasingly under the influence of the English Arts and Crafts designers, and began to conceive a radical new American furniture.

In 1898, he traveled to England and the Continent and then returned to the United States to begin experimenting with the first Craftsman furniture designs. He was attempting to develop a rational style of furniture, based on functionalism and structural truth. His new style was a repudiation of the eclectic, poorly made, over-elaborated furniture common to the late Victorian period. His earliest efforts were not entirely successful expressions of his newly evolving design philosophy, but they did point the way to his later, more fully realized works. The small table shown in Figure 1, which he called the Celandine Tea Table, is a perfect example of his work at this time. Made in 1900, it has a floriform top with curved, shallow relief carving. Its legs are conventionalized expressions of the stems of a plant. It is a long way from the severely rectilinear designs seen in the 1910 catalog, but the tenon-and-key joints holding the flaring cross stretchers to the spindly legs contain the germ of his "structural style of cabinetmaking."

By late 1900 and early 1901, Stickley's work was taking on a new character. It was cross stretchers and massive tenon-and-key joints on each leg, is one example. But in 1909 his catalog showed the beginnings of a new impulse toward even greater simplicity: a lack of structural detail coupled with an increasingly severe rectilinearity. A new single-door china closet and three-drawer serving table appeared for the first time in 1909 (they may be seen on pages 58 and 59 of the 1910 catalog). An equally straight five-drawer chest made its first appearance in 1909 (see page 70 of the catalog).

By 1910, the year the catalog here reprinted was produced, the diversity of the preceding six years was disappearing. Of the Ellis-inspired bowed-side dining-room pieces, only the two-drawer serving table remained (see page 57), but this was the last year it was made. The bowed-side bedroom furniture was still in production (see pages 66 and 67), but every trace of the spindle line was gone. The hexagonal table was continued (see page 48), but shorn of its expressed tenon-and-key joints.

The new pieces making their initial appearance in this catalog reflect the increasing simplification and purity of Stickley's designs we first noticed in 1909. The armchair in Figure 5, which was first produced in this style in 1910 (see page 19), is indicative of this trend toward pure form. Though the chair was originally designed (apparently by Harvey Ellis) in a very different style in 1903, it went through a series of substantial evolutionary changes until it attained its final form in 1910. It is essentially a slat-sided cube, and only the exposed tenons piercing the front legs remind us of Stickley's earlier concern with expressed structure. It is pure, stripped-down form, and in many ways may be seen as the culmination of that development which had begun in 1898 with the Celandine Tea Table.

This armchair, like many of the other Craftsman pieces Stickley made from 1910 until his bankruptcy in 1916, is significant because it draws from the past while pointing toward the future. Its careful joinery is a remnant of the late nineteenth and early twentieth-century crafts tradition of which Stickley was the most vocal American pro-

Figure 5

ing top, gently bowed sides and arched apron, is characteristic of the Ellis-influenced work of the 1904-to-1909 period. Though devoid of inlay, it is also devoid of the kind of structural detail seen in Stickley's pre-Ellis work. Clearly, Ellis left his mark on his employer.

From 1904 through 1909, Stickley's work showed a great diversity. He produced bedroom and dining-room furniture with the same bowed sides and arched aprons seen on this chest of drawers. Starting in August 1905, he produced a line of spindle furniture, which included Wright-influenced high-backed chairs and settees, as well as spindle Morris chairs, library tables, footstools and the like. He also continued to make some pieces with boldly expressed structure. His hexagonal library table (first produced in 1901), with flaring increasingly massive, rectilinear and structural, with the plant-based motifs of his earlier work disappearing. The two-drawer library table in Figure 2, made *circa* 1902, shows how much his work had changed in the two years following the Celandine Tea Table. It is absolutely straight, with massive legs and over-scale structural members. All trace of the earlier decoration based on natural forms is absent, replaced by the severe but vigorous expression of structural members. The straight aprons are joined to the legs by means of mortise and tenon, with four exposed pins holding each joint. The stretchers at both ends are also fastened to the legs with mortise-and-tenon joints, but here the tenons are allowed to pierce the legs and are left exposed. The medial stretcher is held at both ends by tenon-and-key joints.

Stickley's work began to shift again in mid-1903, with the arrival in his workshop of the brilliant, though alcoholic, architect/designer Harvey Ellis. Ellis's work was more purely decorative than Stickley's and showed the unmistakable influence of the most advanced English Arts and Crafts designers of the period, such as C. F. A. Voysey, Baillie Scott and the Glasgow architect Charles Rennie Mackintosh. Avoiding the structural expression characteristic of Stickley's work, Ellis introduced colored inlays to decorate his designs, and created lighter, more delicate forms. The armchair in Figure 3, which dates from late 1903 or early 1904, is one of the pieces Ellis designed for Stickley. It has a high back, with Art Nouveau-derived inlay patterns on the three back slats. The legs and stretchers exhibit delicacy without appearing weak, and the sense of the chair's lightness is enhanced by the graceful arched aprons on the front and side seat rails.

Stickley's Ellis-designed inlay furniture was not commercially successful and its limited production ceased in mid-1904, a few months after Ellis's death. However, it continued to exert an influence on Stickley's designs for many years. Starting in 1904, his furniture began to rely less on boldly articulated structure and grew increasingly simplified. The nine-drawer chest in Figure 4, with its wide overhang-

Figure 3

Figure 4

ponent. It is made of his favorite wood, American white oak, quarter-sawn to show the flake and finished in a dull warm brown. Yet in its uncompromising rectilinearity, its absolute reliance on proportion and unornamented form, it clearly prefigures later design developments. Translated into steel and leather, it could almost pass for an early International Style chair—the plain style that our century has come to call "modern."

L. & J. G. STICKLEY

Leopold and J. George Stickley established their own Arts and Crafts furniture business just a few years after their older brother Gustav had begun his. Their plant was located in Fayetteville, New York, a Syracuse suburb situated a few miles away from Gustav Stickley's Craftsman Workshops in Eastwood. From the first, most L & J. G. Stickley designs were directly derivative of the work of Gustav Stickley, a fact that plagued Gustav throughout his furniture-producing years.

The L & J. G. Stickley catalog repro-

duced in the second part of this volume, though undated, was first issued *circa* 1914. The sketches do not do the furniture justice; photographs would have shown it off to much better advantage. However, the catalog shows Leopold and J. George to have been shrewder marketers than Gustav. The fact that their catalog is undated, while frustrating to those of us who study the furniture, meant that it did not have to be replaced each year. The prices of the furniture were not shown, enabling L. & J. G. Stickley to print separate price lists that could be easily updated. Finally, rather than following Gustav Stickley's practice of organizing a catalog by forms—a page for desks, a page for armchairs, a page for Morris chairs, etc.—they showed pieces grouped as they would be used.

For example, the large armchairs and Morris chairs on pages 22 and 23 are shown with footstools and a smokers' stand. Pages 18 and 19 show armchairs, rockers, a settle and library tables—all the necessary furniture for a den. A catalog organized in this fashion was designed to

Figure 6

create multiple sales by showing furniture within its use context.

Though L & J. G. Stickley did tend to imitate many of Gustav Stickley's designs, their work is not to be disparaged. The construction and finish of the best L. & J. G. Stickley pieces frequently equals Gustav's. However, their work was even more successful when they created their own unique designs. For example, the paneled-side settle in Figure 6 is totally unlike anything ever produced by Gustav Stickley, yet it is without question a first-rate example of American Arts and Crafts furniture. It was first made in 1912, and was still in production when the circa-1914 catalog was issued (see page 24). In terms of design, construction and finish, it is every bit the equal of Craftsman furniture.

L & J. G. Stickley settles in general equal those produced by Gustav Stickley, as do many of their other designs for tabourets,

china closets, sideboards and tall-case clocks.

The republication of these two catalogs is a sign of the mushrooming interest in the American Arts and Crafts Movement of the late nineteenth and early twentieth centuries. The rediscovery and reappraisal of turn-of-the-century decorative arts began in the 1960s and led to the nineteenth-century design exhibition at New York's Metropolitan Museum of Art in 1970. In 1972, Princeton University mounted the landmark exhibition *The Arts and Crafts Movement in America 1876–1916*. This pioneering show, more than any other single event, brought about the reawakening of interest in this fertile period.

DAVID M. CATHERS

Introduction Photo Credits: Figure 3, courtesy of Jordan Volpe Gallery; all other photos by H. Peter Curran, New York.

Catalogue of
CRAFTSMAN
FURNITURE

Made by

GUSTAV STICKLEY at
THE CRAFTSMAN WORKSHOPS
EASTWOOD, N. Y.

P. O. Address
SYRACUSE, N. Y.

Craftsman Show Rooms:
41 West 34th Street, New York
470 Boylston Street, Boston

The Craftsman idea makes for the development in this country of an art and architecture which shall express the spirit of the American people; for the creation of conditions which shall provide the best home environment for our children; for a form of industrial education which will enable men and women to earn their own living.

CRAFTSMAN FURNITURE

NYBODY who knows Craftsman furniture has no difficulty in perceiving that the principles upon which it is based are honesty and simplicity. This is quite true, for when I first began to make it I did so because I felt that the badly-constructed, over-ornate, meaningless furniture that was turned out in such quantities by the factories was not only bad in itself, but that its presence in the homes of the people was an influence that led directly away from the sound qualities which make an honest man and a good citizen. It seemed to me that we were getting to be a thoughtless, extravagant people, fond of show and careless of real value, and that one way to counteract this national tendency was to bring about, if possible, a different standard of what was desirable in our homes.

I suppose it was because I began as a farmer boy and got my training for the work I was ultimately to do by doing as a matter of course the thing which had to be done, that I grew up with the habit of going at things in a natural way. The farmer boy is not given to theorizing about his work, but he soon learns to accept without question the fact that certain things have to be done and that the best way is for him to get right at it and get them done as soon as possible.

Therefore, when the idea came to me that the thing for me to do was to make better and simpler furniture, I naturally went at it in the most direct way. Having been for many years a furniture manufacturer, I was, of course, familiar with all the traditional styles, and in trying to make the kind of furniture which I thought was needed in our homes, I had no idea of attempting to create a new style, but merely tried to make furniture which would be simple, durable, comfortable and fitted for the place it was to occupy and the work it had to do. It seemed to me that the only way to do this was to cut loose from all tradition and to do away with all needless ornamentation, returning to plain principles of construction and applying them to the making of simple, strong, comfortable furniture, and I firmly believe that Craftsman furniture is the concrete expression of this idea.

Because of the sturdiness and beauty of our American white oak, I chose it as the best wood for the kind of furniture I had in mind, and the "style," such as it was, developed naturally from the character of the wood and the application to it of the most direct principles of construction. The result was that I soon found that there was a quality in my plain furniture which took hold of nearly all thinking people as it had taken hold of me, and that in giving expression to what might have been considered an impractical ideal under present-day conditions, I had hit upon an idea which was destined to have a far greater success than even I had hoped for it.

The first pieces of Craftsman furniture were completed in 1898 and then for two years more I worked steadily over the development of forms, the adjustment of proportions and the search for a finish which would protect the wood and mellow it in color without sacrificing its natural woody quality. Then in 1900 I introduced Craftsman furniture to the public at large by exhibiting it at the Furniture Exposition in Grand Rapids, Michigan. The result showed that I had not been mistaken in supposing that this,—the first original expression of American thought in furniture,—would appeal strongly to the directness and common sense. of the American people. From the time of that first exhibition Craftsman furniture grew rapidly in favor, and after the Pan American Exposition in 1901 its success was assured.

BEGINNING OF METAL AND LEATHER WORK

BUT this success carried with it the obligation to go on and develop still further the basic principles which had found expression in the furniture. The first need was for metal trim which would harmonize in character with the furniture, as none of the glittering, fragile metal then in vogue was possible in connection with its straight severe lines and plain surfaces. So I opened a metal work department in The Craftsman Workshops, and there we made plain, strong handles, pulls, hinges and escutcheons of iron, copper and brass, so designed and made that each article fulfilled as simply and directly as possible the purpose for which it was intended, and so finished that the natural quality of each metal was shown frankly as was the quality of the wood against which it was placed. Also,—for Craftsman furniture is very exacting in its requirements,—leather was needed for cushions, table tops and seats for chairs and settles, and sturdy fabrics interesting in color, weave and texture, had to be found for the same purpose. This necessitated a further expansion to take in the special treatment of leathers so that they harmonize with the Craftsman idea in maintaining all their leathery quality unimpaired, while giving long service under hard wear; and also to include a fabric department, that the textiles used in connection with the furniture would be sure to have the qualities that would harmonize with it.

GROWTH OF OUR DECORATIVE SCHEME

THE fact that the furniture so imperatively demanded the right kind of metal work and fabrics naturally opened the way to a more extended use of these departments in the making of things intended for general furnishings. While Craftsman furniture is very friendly in its nature and fits in comfortably with any good simple scheme of interior decoration and furnishing, it yet holds out a strong temptation to develop an entire scheme of furnishing along the same lines. So we began in the metal shop to make electric lighting fixtures, fireplace fittings, trays, candlesticks and all manner of useful household articles, designed on the same general principles as the furniture and therefore just as essentially a part of one general scheme of furnishing. The fabrics in their turn were made into curtains, portières, pillows, scarfs, centerpieces and the like, and decorated with needlework and appliqué in strong simple designs and colorings which belonged to the oaken furniture as naturally as the leaves on a tree belong to the trunk. So, step by step, we grew naturally into the designing and arranging, first of rooms, then of entire schemes of interior decoration, and lastly the planning and building of the whole house.

THE INDIVIDUALITY OF CRAFTSMAN FURNITURE

AS I have already said, Craftsman furniture is built for all manner of uses and its construction is so thorough that it will last for the lifetime of the oak of which it is made, which means the lifetime of several generations of men. Being designed upon the most natural lines and made in the most natural way, there is little room for change in the style, and that the style itself has made good its appeal to the American people is best proven by the fact that, during the twelve years it has been upon the market, it has remained unchanged, except for such modifications and improvements as evidence a healthy growth along normal lines of development. It is impossible to get far away from the structural lines which declare the purpose and use of the piece, and the proportions that best serve that purpose and use are the proportions which it should have. As to the matter of decoration, it will grow of itself in time, for true decoration is always the natural expression of the thought and desire of the people who own and use the things made, combined with the desire of the craftsman to express his own idea of beauty. I am so sure of this that I have been content to leave the furniture absolutely plain until the form of decoration which inevitably belongs to it shall come.

HOW WE FINISH CRAFTSMAN FURNITURE

OF COURSE, a great deal depends upon the finish which is given the oak of which it is made. This is a case where art must come to the aid of nature, because to leave the wood in the purely natural state would be to leave it exposed to all manner of soil and stain from wear. Also, the natural color of new oak is rather uninteresting; it needs age and exposure to give it the depth and mellowness which we associate with this wood. So, while our whole object is to keep the wood looking entirely natural in its possession of all the qualities which belong to oak, this can be done only by the most careful treatment. Some time ago it was discovered that the fumes of ammonia would, within a very short time, darken white oak naturally, giving it the appearance which ordinarily would result from age and use. Therefore, as soon as a piece of Craftsman furniture is made, it is first moistened all over to open the pores, and then put into an air-tight compartment, on the floor of which are placed basins of very strong (26%) ammonia. The time usually demanded for this fuming is forty-eight hours, but that is varied according to the wood and the depth of color required. After the fuming the wood is carefully sand papered by hand until all the loose fiber is rubbed away and every trace of roughness removed. Then comes the final finish. For years I worked and experimented to find something that would leave the furniture entirely free from the hard glaze given by the use of shellac or varnish and yet would completely protect it, not only from soil or stain but also from the atmospheric changes which cause it to shrink or swell. It was a difficult problem,—that of finding a method of finishing which would preserve all the woody quality of the oak without sacrificing the protection needed to make it "stand" under widely varying climatic conditions,—and it is only recently that I hit upon a solution which satisfies me. I found that all that is required to develop the best qualities of oak is to so ripen and mellow the wood that the full value of its natural color is brought out, as well as the individual beauty of texture and grain. The final finish we give it adds very little color, as our aim is rather to develop than to alter the natural tone of the wood, which always appears as an undertone below the surface tint. By the use of this finish we give the oak three different tones, all of which belong essentially to the wood. One is a light soft brown that is not unlike the hue of the frost-bitten oak leaf; another is the rich nut-brown tone which time gives to very old oak; and the third is a delicate gray that gives to the brown of the wood a silvery sheen such as might be produced by the action of the sun and wind. For the last rubbing we use the "Craftsman Wood Luster," which is not a varnish or a polish, but which gives a soft satiny luster to the surface of the wood. When that surface is worn or soiled with use it may be fully restored—if the soil does not penetrate beyond the surface—by wiping it off with a piece of cheesecloth dampened with the Wood Luster and then rubbing it dry with a fresh cloth.

THE CRAFTSMAN LEATHERS

IN THE selection of materials for covering our chairs and settles, we give the preference to the Craftsman leathers, which are especially prepared to harmonize with the design and finish of our furniture. These leathers are of three kinds—Hard and Soft Leather and Sheepskin, all finished by a process of our own, and each satisfactory in its place. The Hard and Soft Leathers are produced by the use of different methods in tanning cattle hides, by which one is made much like sole leather in stiffness and durability, and is given a smooth, hard surface, while the other is rendered soft and pliable, with a surface possessing texture enough to give an excellent effect when dull-finished. Hard Leather is used for table tops and for chair and settle seats where the leather is stretched over the seat rails and nailed on. Soft Leather is used for slip seats in chairs and for loose seat cushions in settles, where the size of the cushion requires a large hide. Sheepskin is the softest and most flexible of all our leathers, and seems to me to be best adapted to covering pillows and loose seat and back cushions for chairs, where the skins can be used without piecing.

My constant experimenting with finishes has included the treatment of leather as well as wood, and my recent success with wood finishes suggested a way to improve the leather as well. The result is that I have not only found a method by which all these leathers are made waterproof, but also I have been able to do away with what so far has been the weak point of Sheepskin, for I am now dressing the skins in such a way that they are entirely free from any tendency to check or craze. Naturally, their wearing quality is greatly improved, and in addition to this I have been able to obtain a beauty of color and a softness of surface that, so far as I know, has never been equaled. No artificial graining is used, but the natural grain of each kind of leather is left to show its full value.

CUSHIONS AND PILLOWS

ALL our loose spring-seat cushions for chairs and settles are made so that the shape will be retained even under the hardest wear. These cushions are made over stout wood frames which are carefully fitted to each piece, and have exactly the same appearance as the ordinary loose cushions, except that the frame upon which the cushion is built slips just inside the frame of the chair, so that the seat, although removable, is always in place. Its construction not only makes it more comfortable than the ordinary cushion, but keeps it from ever getting out of shape or wearing into hollows like the ordinary stuffed cushions. Where the backs of chairs require loose cushions, they are made with equal care and filled with Java floss.

LEATHER-COVERED TABLES

WITH some of our more massive tables, we have been able to obtain an added interest by covering the top with hard leather, finished in a color that blends with and emphasizes the tone of the wood. Naturally, we use only a single large hide in covering a table top, so that the surface is perfect, and the great spread of leather, showing the most charming play of varied tones over the glossy surface,—which yet retains all the leathery quality as an undertone,—gives an effect of rich and sober excellence to the piece that makes it easily the center of attraction among the furnishings of a living room or a large and well-appointed library. We quote in the catalogue the prices of both wood-top and leather-top; but for those that are best left all in wood, we quote no price in leather.

OUR HARD LEATHER CHAIR SEAT

ALL our leather-seated chairs, which have not either slip seats or spring-seat cushions, are made with firm, flat seats of hard leather, stretched tightly over the rails. This seat has unlimited durability. The foundation is made of very thick, firm canvas, stretched tightly over the seat-rails and nailed underneath. Over this heavy webbing is woven as closely as the width of the strands will permit, and just enough padding is laid over the top to give a smooth surface above the webbing—but not enough to interfere with the perfect flatness of the seat. Then the hard leather, stiff and firm as sole leather, is stretched over the rails, wrapped around and nailed on the inside. The square-headed nails are used only at the corners, where they fasten down the leather that is cut around the posts.

BENT ROCKERS

ALL the rockers now used on Craftsman rocking chairs are cut straight with the grain of the wood and then bent with steam pressure by bending machines. This precaution makes the rocker as strong as any other part of the chair and entirely does away with the danger of breaking that exists when the rocker is cut on a curve that partly crosses the grain.

HOW TO IDENTIFY CRAFTSMAN FURNITURE

FROM its first success in 1900, the popularity achieved by Craftsman furniture was the signal to an army of imitators who saw in it what they considered a novelty that would prove to be a notable money-maker. These manufacturers at once began to turn out large quantities of furniture which was designed in what seemed to them the same style. But failing to comprehend my reasons for giving to Craftsman furniture forms that were plain and almost primitive, they naturally seized upon this primitiveness as a fad which might be profitable and exaggerated it into intentional crudeness. This imitation has grown instead of decreased with the passing of time, and while in one sense it is the best evidence of the popularity and stability of the Craftsman style, in another it creates confusion which at times is annoying. Restrained by law from the use of my registered name, "Craftsman," these manufacturers get as near to it as they can and variously style their products "Mission," "Hand-Craft," "Arts and Crafts," "Crafts-Style," "Roycroft," and "Quaint." To add to the confusion, some of the most persistent of these imitators bear the same name as myself and what is called "Stickley furniture" is frequently, through misrepresentation on the part of salesmen and others, sold as "Craftsman furniture or just the same thing."

Purchasers should bear this in mind when selecting furniture, and if they desire to get the genuine Craftsman furniture, they should remember that by this name alone it is known, and that it is sold only by the dealers whose names appear in the list of associates printed in this catalogue and in each issue of THE CRAFTSMAN Magazine. Furthermore, it should be borne in mind that each piece of Craftsman furniture is not only tagged with the name "Craftsman," but is stamped with my registered shop mark—a joiner's compass of ancient make, enclosing the motto "Als ik Kan," and bearing my own signature below. Also, each piece bears the price tag as shown here. This tag is attached before the piece leaves my workshops, for the price of my work is fixed only by myself. The freight charges for the transportation of furniture to the other side of the continent make it necessary to have two price lists, one of which obtains in all parts of the country east of Denver, while the other applies to all points west of Denver, including the Pacific Coast.

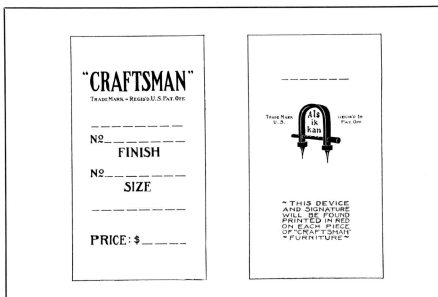

OUR GUARANTEE TO PURCHASERS

THE making of Craftsman furniture has come to be such an important part of my life, and personally I care so much for the things I have made, that it makes a great deal of difference to me whether or not the people who own and use it have toward it a thoroughly satisfied and friendly feeling. My idea of it is that the first cost of the furniture to the purchaser is only a part of its value, which will steadily increase with age and use. It is not a question of buying a chair or a table that will fall to pieces or go out of fashion in a few years, so that it has to be replaced with another that in time suffers the same fate, but of buying a piece of furniture that will be a permanent part of the home surroundings and that in fifty or a hundred years will be worth many times its first cost, for the time is coming when good oak furniture will be as valuable on account of its permanent worth and also of its scarcity as the fine old Spanish mahogany pieces are now. For these reasons I wish every purchaser of Craftsman furniture clearly to understand that I prefer to take back or make good any piece that is defective in any way, or for some other reason is not entirely satisfactory.

No. 212

Settle,
Hard Leather
Seat - - $25.00

Height of Back
from Floor 36 in.
Height of Seat
from Floor 17 in.
Length 48 in.
Depth 21 in.

No. 311½

Arm Rocker, Hard Leather
Seat - - - - - - - - $12.50

Height of Back from Floor 34 in.
Height of Seat from Floor 15 in.
Size of Seat 20 in. wide, 19 in. deep

No. 311 (Same Design and
Dimensions as No. 311½)
Arm Rocker, Rush Seat - $11.00

No. 312½

Arm Chair, Hard Leather
Seat - - - - - - - - $12.50

Height of Back from Floor 37 in.
Height of Seat from Floor 18 in.
Size of Seat 20 in. wide, 19 in. deep

No. 312 (Same Design and
Dimensions as No. 312½)
Arm Chair, Rush Seat - - $11.00

No. 317

Arm Rocker, Spring Seat
Cushion, Sheepskin - - - $17.00

Height of Back from Floor 38 in.
Height of Seat from Floor 15 in.
Size of Seat 21 in. wide, 19 in. deep

No. 318

Arm Chair, Spring Seat
Cushion, Sheepskin - - - $17.00

Height of Back from Floor 38 in.
Height of Seat from Floor 18 in.
Size of Seat 21 in. wide, 19 in. deep

No. 219

Settle, Spring Seat Cushion,
Soft Leather - - - - - $48.00

Height of Back from Floor 39 in.
Height of Seat from Floor 18 in.
Length 72 in.
Depth 23 in.

No. 218 (Design same as No. 219)

Settle, Spring Seat Cushion,
Soft Leather - - - - - $35.00

Height of Back from Floor 39 in.
Height of Seat from Floor 18 in.
Length 48 in.
Depth 23 in.

No. 326

Arm Chair, Loose Seat
Cushion, Sheepskin - - - $15.00

Height of Back from Floor 37 in.
Height of Seat from Floor 18 in.
Size of Seat 19½ in. wide, 18 in. deep

No. 325

Arm Rocker, Loose Seat
Cushion, Sheepskin - - - $15.00

Height of Back from Floor 36 in.
Height of Seat from Floor 14 in.
Size of Seat 19½ in. wide, 18 in deep

No. 208

Settle, Spring Seat Cushion,
Soft Leather - - - - - $78.00

Height of Back from Floor 29 in.

Height of Seat from Floor 16 in.
Length 76 in.
Depth 32 in.
Sheepskin Pillows extra $8.00 each

No. 226

Settle, Spring Seat Cushion,
Soft Leather - - - - - $50.00

Height of Back from Floor 29 in.

Height of Seat from Floor 16 in.
Length 60 in.
Depth 30 in.

Sheepskin Pillows extra $8.00 each

No. 225

Settle, Spring Seat Cushion,
Soft Leather - - - - - $68.00

Height of Back from Floor 29 in.

Height of Seat from Floor 16 in.
Length 79 in.
Depth 31 in.

Sheepskin Pillows extra $8.00 each

No. 319

Arm Rocker, Spring Seat
Cushion, Sheepskin - - - $27.00

Height of Back from Floor 38 in.
Height of Seat from Floor 15 in.
Size of Seat 21 in. wide, 25 in. deep

No. 320

Arm Chair, Spring Seat
Cushion, Sheepskin - - - $27.00

Height of Back from Floor 42 in.
Height of Seat from Floor 16 in.
Size of Seat 21 in. wide, 25 in. deep

No. 210

Settle, Spring Seat Cushion,
Soft Leather - - - - - $96.50

Height of Back from Floor 36 in.

Height of Seat from Floor 16 in.
Length 84 in.
Depth 34 in.

Sheepskin Pillows extra $8.00 each

No. 323
Arm Rocker, Spring Seat
Cushion, Sheepskin - - - $29.00

Height of Back from Floor 40 in.
Height of Seat from Floor 15 in.
Size of Seat 22 in. wide, 25 in. deep

No. 324
Arm Chair, Spring Seat
Cushion, Sheepskin - - - $29.00

Height of Back from Floor 41 in.
Height of Seat from Floor 16 in.
Size of Seat 21 in. wide, 25 in. deep

No. 222
Settle, Spring Seat Cushion,
Soft Leather - - - - - $90.00

Height of Back from Floor 36 in.

Height of Seat from Floor 16 in
Length 80 in.
Depth 33 in.
Sheepskin Pillows extra $8.00 each

No. 336

Reclining Chair, Adjustable
Back, Spring Seat Cushion,
Sheepskin - - - - - - $31.50

Height of Back from Floor 40 in.
Height of Seat from Floor 16 in.
Size of Seat 22 in. wide, 23 in. deep

No. 396

Chair, Spring Seat Cushion,
Sheepskin - - - - - - $38.00

Height of Back from Floor 41 in.
Height of Seat from Floor 16 in.
Size of Seat 23 in. wide, 28 in. deep

No. 332

Reclining Chair, Adjustable
Back, Spring Seat Cushion,
Sheepskin - - - - $33.00

Height of Back from Floor
40 in.

Height of Seat from Floor
16 in.

Size of Seat 23 in. wide, 27
in. deep

No. 369

Reclining Chair, Adjustable
Back, Spring Seat Cushion,
Sheepskin - - - - $37.00

Height of Back from Floor
40 in.

Height of Seat from Floor
15 in.

Size of Seat 23 in. wide, 27
in. deep

No. 205

Hall Settle, Spring Seat Cushion
Soft Leather - - - - - $35.00

Height of Back from Floor 30 in.
Height of Seat from Floor 16 in.
Length 56 in.
Depth 22 in.

No. 346

Reclining Chair, Adjustable
Back, Spring Seat Cushion
Sheepskin - - - - - $25.50

Height of Back from Floor 41
in.
Height of Seat from Floor 16
in.
Size of Seat 21 in. wide, 24 in
deep.

No. 397

Arm Rocker, Spring
Seat Cushion, Sheep-
skin - - - - $14.50

Height of Back from
Floor 43 in.
Height of Seat from
Floor 15 in.
Size of Seat 20 in.
wide, 18 in. deep

No. 331

Arm Chair, Spring Seat
Cushion, Sheepskin - $30.00

Height of Back from Floor
30 in.
Height of Seat from Floor
16 in.
Size of Seat 23 in. wide, 26
in. deep

No. 366

Arm Chair, Hard Leather
Seat - - - - - - - - $11.00

Height of Back from Floor 39 in.
Height of Seat from Floor 18. in.
Size of Seat 20 in. wide, 17 in. deep

No. 365

Arm Rocker, Hard Leather
Seat - - - - - - - - $11.00

Height of Back from Floor 38 in.
Height of Seat from Floor 15 in.
Size of Seat 20 in. wide, 17 in. deep

No. 523

Bookcase - - $26.00

Height 44 in.
Length over all 39 in.
Depth 12 in.
Stationary Shelves on
Line of Mullions

These bookcases are made in five sizes and have stationary shelves on the line of the mullions. They are all the same design, the only difference being in No. 715, which is made with the single door

No. 715

Bookcase, One Door - - $30.00

Height 56 in.
Width 36 in.
Depth 13 in.

No. 716

Bookcase, Two Doors - - $37.00

Height 56 in.
Width 42 in.
Depth 13 in.

No. 717

Bookcase, Two Doors - - - $41.00

Height 56 in.
Width 48 in.
Depth 13 in.

No. 718

Bookcase, Two Doors - - - $45.00

Height 56 in.
Width 54 in.
Depth 13 in.

No. 719

Bookcase, Two Doors - - - $49.00

Height 56 in.
Width 60 in.
Depth 13 in.

No. 713

Roll Top Desk - - - - $115.00

Height to Top 30 in.
Height over all 46 in.
Length 60 in.
Depth 32 in.
Flat Lock on Roll
Arm Slides on Sides
Automatic Lock on Drawers

No. 363

Desk Chair, Hard Leather
Seat - - - - - - - - $23.00

Height of Back from Seat 19 in.
Size of Seat 22 in. wide, 19 in. deep
Height Adjustable
Screw and Spring

No. 364

Arm Chair,
Hard Leather
Seat - - $21.00

Height of Back
from Floor 37 in.
Height of Seat
from Floor 18 in.
Size of Seat 22
in. wide, 19 in.
deep

The Back is made of a Double Band of Hard Leather suspended
between the Two Posts
Seat and Back both Studded with Nails

No. 360

Arm Chair - - - - - - $18.00

Hard Leather Seat and Back Studded with Nails
Height of Back from Floor 37 in.
Height of Seat from Floor 18 in.
Size of Seat 21 in. wide, 18 in. deep

No. 361

Desk Chair - - - - - $23.00

Hard Leather Seat and Back Studded with Nails
Height of Back from Seat 19 in.
Size of Seat 21 in. wide, 18 in. deep
Height Adjustable
Screw and Spring

Desk Chair without Arms (Screw and Spring) is shown on Page 81.

No. 713
Roll Top Desk (Open)

No. 720

Desk   - - - $24.50

Height 30 in.
Width 38 in.
Depth 22 in.
Depth of Cabinet 8 in.
Height of Cabinet 8 in.

No. 711

Library Table or Desk, Wood
Top - - - - - - - - $70.00
Hard Leather Top - - - 93.00

Height 30 in.
Length 60 in.
Width 32 in.
Arm Slide on each Side
Thickness of Top 1¼ in.

No. 96

Letter Case - - - - - - $2.50
Height 6½ in.
Length 12 in.
Depth 7 in.
Bottom covered with Ooze Leather

No. 712

Desk, with Cabinet Top - $90.00

Height 30 in.
Length 60 in.
Depth 32 in.

Arm Slide on each Side
Height of Cabinets 6 in.
Length of Cabinets 18 in.
Depth of Cabinets 12 in.

No. 708

Desk - - - $25.00

Height 30 in.
Width 40 in.
Depth 22 **in.**
Depth of Shelf 10 in.
Height of Cabinet 6 in.
Depth of Cabinet 5 in.

No. 731

Desk - - - - - $28.00

Height 42 in.
Width 30 in.
Depth 15 in.
Writing Space 27½ in. wide,
23 in. deep

No. 731

Desk (Open)

No. 728

Desk - - - - - $20.00

Height 39 in.
Width 30 in.
Depth 14 in.
Writing Space 27½ in. wide,
21½ in. deep

No. 728

Desk (Open)

No. 729

Writing Desk - - $39.00

Height 43 in.
Width 36 in.
Depth 14 in.
Writing Space 34 in. wide,
18 in. deep

No. 729

Writing Desk (Closed)

No. 732

Desk - - - - - $32.00

Height 42 in.
Width 32 in.
Depth 14 in.
Writing Space 30 in. wide,
20 in. deep

No. 732
Desk (Open)

No. 706

Desk　- - - - -　$26.00

Height 44 in.
Width 30 in.
Depth 11 in.
Writing Space 23 in. wide,
17 in. deep

No. 94

Scrap Basket - - - $4.75

Height 14 in.
Diameter at Top 12 in.
Wrought Iron Hoops

No. 706
Desk (Open)

No. 709

Desk, Wood Top - - - $38.00
Hard Leather Top - - - 48.00
Height 29 in.
Length 42 in.
Width 24 in.

No. 710 (Same Design as No. 709)

Desk, Wood Top - - - $45.00
Hard Leather Top - - - 57.00
Height 30 in.
Length 48 in.
Width 29 in.

No. 608

Tea Table - - - - - - $7.50
Height 26 in.
Diameter of Top 24 in.
Distance of Shelf from Floor 12 in.

No. 605

Telephone Stand - - - - $5.50
Height 29 in.
Top 14 in. x 14 in.

No. 314

Arm Chair, rush or soft leather slip
seat - - - - - - - - $9.00

Height of Back from Floor 40 in.
Height of Seat from Floor 18 in.
Size of Seat 21 in. wide, 18 in. deep
Seat tapered in Back to 19 in.

No. 313

Arm Rocker, rush or soft leather
slip seat - - - - - - - $9.00

Height of Back from Floor 38 in.
Height of Seat from Floor 15 in.
Size of Seat 21 in. wide, 18 in. deep
Seat tapered in Back to 19 in.

No. 307

Rocker, rush or soft leather slip
seat - - - - - - - - $4.75

Height of Back from Floor 36 in.
Height of Seat from Floor 15 in.
Size of Seat 17 in. wide, 15 in. deep
Seat tapered in Back to 15 in.

No. 308

Chair, rush or soft leather slip
seat - - - - - - - - $4.75

Height of Back from Floor 40 in.
Height of Seat from Floor 18 in.
Size of Seat 17 in. wide, 15 in. deep
Seat tapered in Back to 15 in.

No. 306 (Same Design and Dimensions as No. 306½)
Chair, Rush Seat - - $5.50

No. 305 (Same Design and Dimensions as No. 305½)
Rocker, Rush Seat - - $5.50

No. 306½

Chair, Hard Leather Seat - $6.50

Height of Back from Floor 36 in.
Height of Seat from Floor 18 in.
Size of Seat 16 in. x 16 in.

No. 305½

Sewing Rocker, Hard Leather Seat - - - - - - - - $6.50

Height of Back from Floor 31 in.
Height of Seat from Floor 14 in.
Size of Seat 16 in. x 16 in.

No. 309 (Same Design and Dimensions as No. 309½)
Arm Rocker, Rush Seat - $9.00

No. 310 (Same Design and Dimensions as No. 310½)
Arm Chair, Rush Seat - - $9.00

No. 309½
Arm Rocker, Hard Leather Seat - - - - - - - $10.50

Height of Back from Floor 32 in.
Height of Seat from Floor 15 in.
Size of Seat 20 in. wide, 19 in. deep

No. 310½
Arm Chair, Hard Leather Seat - - - - - - - $10.50

Height of Back from Floor 36 in.
Height of Seat from Floor 18 in.
Size of Seat 20 in. wide, 19 in. deep

No. 72

Magazine
Cabinet - - - $12.00

Height 42 in
Width 22 in.
Depth 13 in.

No. 79

Magazine
Cabinet   - - $8.50

Height 40 in.
Width 14 in.
Depth 10 in.

No. 670

Music Rack - - - - - $14.00

Height 39 in.
Width 25 in.
Depth 15 in.
Distance between Shelves 8 in.

No. 328

Chair, Loose Seat Cushion,
Sheepskin - - - - - - $10.00

Height of Back from Floor 37 in.
Height of Seat from Floor 18 in.
Size of Seat 17½ in. wide, 16 in. deep

No. 327

Rocker, Loose Seat Cushion,
Sheepskin - - - - - - $10.00

Height of Back from Floor 32 in.
Height of Seat from Floor 14 in.
Size of Seat 17½ in. wide, 16 in. deep

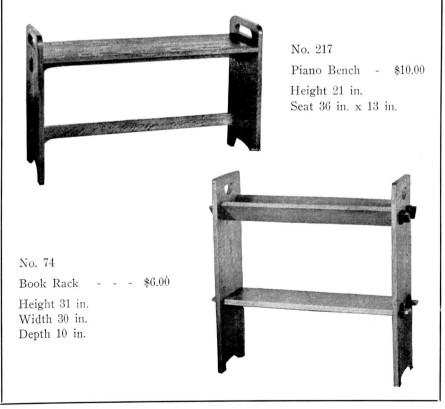

No. 217

Piano Bench - $10.00

Height 21 in.
Seat 36 in. x 13 in.

No. 74

Book Rack - - - $6.00

Height 31 in.
Width 30 in.
Depth 10 in.

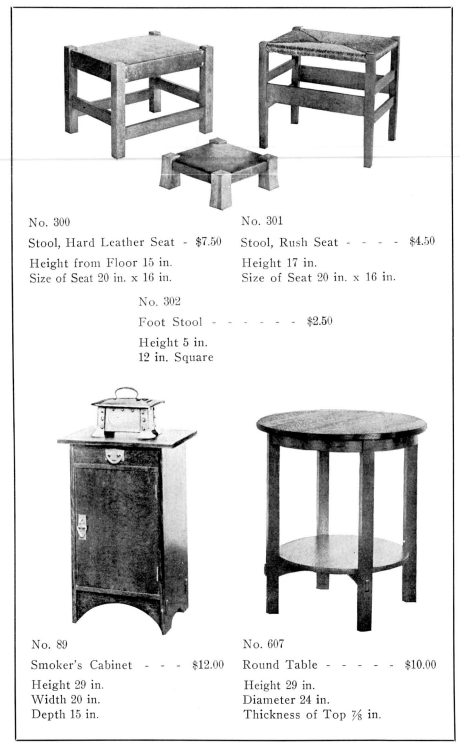

No. 300

Stool, Hard Leather Seat - $7.50

Height from Floor 15 in.
Size of Seat 20 in. x 16 in.

No. 301

Stool, Rush Seat - - - - $4.50

Height 17 in.
Size of Seat 20 in. x 16 in.

No. 302

Foot Stool - - - - - - $2.50

Height 5 in.
12 in. Square

No. 89

Smoker's Cabinet - - - $12.00

Height 29 in.
Width 20 in.
Depth 15 in.

No. 607

Round Table - - - - - $10.00

Height 29 in.
Diameter 24 in.
Thickness of Top ⅞ in.

No. 601

Tabouret - $2.50

Height 16 in.
Diameter 14 in.

No. 602

Tabouret - $3.00

Height 18 in.
Diameter 16 in.

No. 603

Tabouret - $3.75

Height 20 in.
Diameter 18 in.

No. 604

Tea Table - $4.75

Height 26 in.
Diameter 20 in.

No. 654

Tea Table - $6.25

Height 28 in.
Diameter 24 in.

No. 660

Plant Stand - - - - - - $4.50

Height 20 in.
Top 18 in. x 18 in.

No. 611

Square Table   - - - - - $9.00

Height 29 in.
Top 24 in. x 24 in.
Thickness of Top 1 in.

No. 95

Shirt-Waist Box - - - - $16.00

Height 16 in.
Length 32 in.
Width 17 in.
Cedar Lined
Hand Wrought Lifts
Yale mortise lock

This box is very convenient if placed where it can be used as a window or fireside seat in a bedroom

No. 70

Music Cabinet, Paneled
Door - - - - - - $20.00

Height 46 in.
Width 20 in.
Depth 16 in.
Adjustable Shelves

No. 70

Music Cabinet, Amber Glass
Door - - - - - - - - $24.00

Height 46 in.
Width 20 in.
Depth 16 in.
Stationary Shelves on the line of
the Mullions

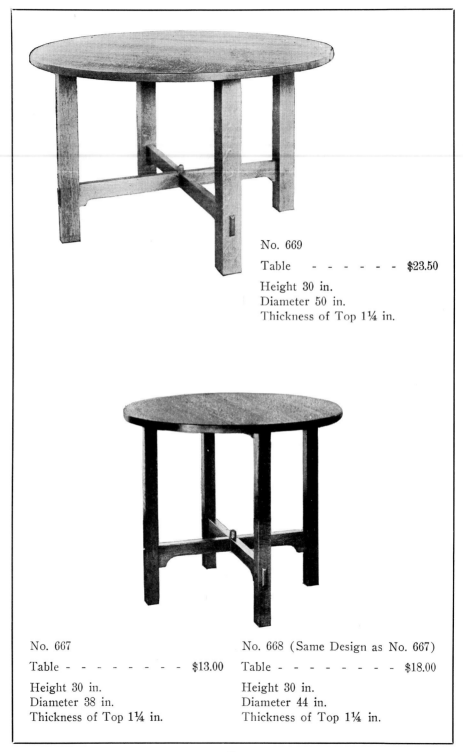

No. 669

Table - - - - - - $23.50

Height 30 in.
Diameter 50 in.
Thickness of Top 1¼ in.

No. 667

Table - - - - - - - - $13.00

Height 30 in.
Diameter 38 in.
Thickness of Top 1¼ in.

No. 668 (Same Design as No. 667)

Table - - - - - - - - $18.00

Height 30 in.
Diameter 44 in.
Thickness of Top 1¼ in.

No. 633

Library Table, Wood Top - $30.00

Hard Leather Top - - - 48.00

Height 29 in.
Diameter 44 in.
Thickness of Top 1⅝ in.

No. 626

Table - - - - $19.50

Height 30 in.
Diameter 40 in.
Thickness of Top 1 in.

No. 673

Round Drop-Leaf Table - $20.00

Height 29 in.
Diameter, Opened 44 in.
Closed 44 in. long, 14 in. wide
Thickness of Top 1 in.

No. 671

Round Drop-Leaf Table - $14.00

Height 29 in.
Diameter, Opened 32 in.
Closed 32 in. long, 10 in. wide
Thickness of Top ⅞ in.

No. 672 (Same Design as No. 671)

Round Drop-Leaf Table - $18.00

Height 29 in.
Diameter, Opened 38 in.
Closed 38 in. long, 12 in. wide
Thickness of Top ⅞ in.

No. 650

Table   -   -   -   -   -   -   - $14.00

Height 30 in.
Length 36 in.
Width 24 in.
Thickness of Top ⅞ in.

No. 649

Table   -   -   -   -   -   - $10.00

Height 30 in.
Length 30 in.
Width 20 in.
Thickness of Top ⅞ in.

No. 651

Table, Wood Top - - - $24.00
Hard Leather Top - - - 38.00

Height 29 in.
Length 48 in.
Width 30 in.
Thickness of Top ⅞ in.

No. 90

Revolving Book Rack - - $5.00

Height 9 in.
12 in. square
Bottom is covered with Ooze Leather

No. 644

Table - - - - - - - $12.00

Height 29 in.
Diameter 30 in.
Thickness of Top ⅞ in.

No. 645 (Same Design as No. 644)

Table - - - - - - - $16.00

Height 29 in.
Diameter 36 in.
Thickness of Top ⅞ in.

No. 646 (Same Design as No. 644)

Table - - - - - - - $20.00

Height 29 in.
Diameter 40 in.
Thickness of Top 1 in.

No. 652

Library Table - - - - - $14.00

Height 30 in.
Length 36 in.
Width 24 in.
Thickness of Top ⅞ in.

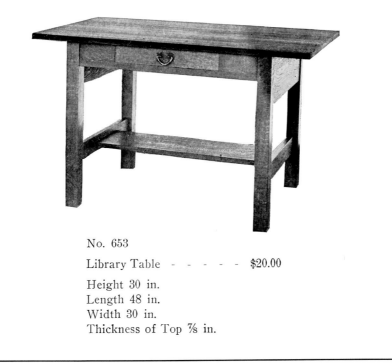

No. 653

Library Table - - - - - $20.00

Height 30 in.
Length 48 in.
Width 30 in.
Thickness of Top ⅞ in.

No. 616

Library Table,
Hard Leather
Top   - $58.50
Wood Top 42.00

Height 30 in.
Length 54 in.
Width 32 in.
Thickness of Top
1 in.

No. 615 (Same Design as No. 614)

Library Table, Wood Top - $35.00
Hard Leather Top - - -   49.00

Height 30 in.
Length 48 in.
Width 30 in.
Thickness of Top 1 in.

No. 614

Library Table,
Wood Top - $26.00
Hard Leather
Top - - - $38.50

Height 30 in.
Length 42 in.
Width 30 in.
Thickness of Top
1 in.

No. 613 (Same Design as No. 614)

Library Table - - - - - $19.00

Height 30 in.
Length 36 in.
Width 24 in.
Thickness of Top ⅞ in.

No. 647

Lunch Table - $14.00

Height 30 in.
Length 40 in.
Width 28 in.
Thickness of Top 1 in.

No. 637

Library Table, Wood Top - $25.00
Hard Leather Top - - - 38.00

Height 29 in.
Length 48 in.
Width 30 in.
Thickness of Top 1 in.

No. 623

Table - - - - - - - - $35.00

Height 30 in.
Length 66 in.
Width 36 in.
Thickness of Top 1½ in.

No. 624

Library Table,
Wood Top $41.50
Hard Leather
Top - - $58.50

Height 29 in.
Hexagonal 48 in.
Thickness of Top
1⅝ in.

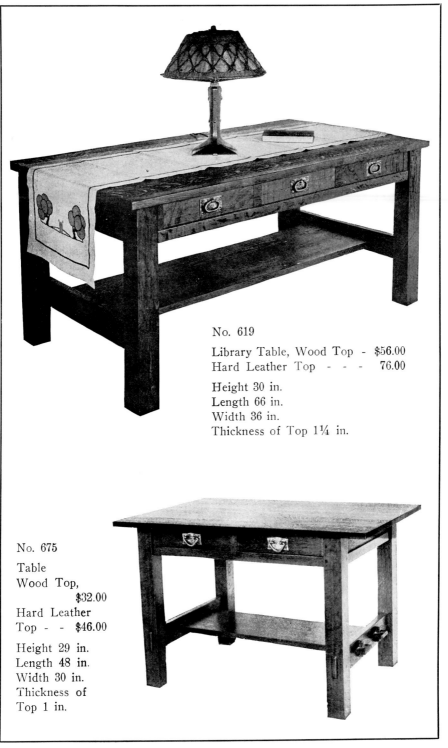

No. 619

Library Table, Wood Top - $56.00
Hard Leather Top - - - 76.00

Height 30 in.
Length 66 in.
Width 36 in.
Thickness of Top 1¼ in.

No. 675

Table
Wood Top,
$32.00
Hard Leather
Top - - $46.00

Height 29 in.
Length 48 in.
Width 30 in.
Thickness of
Top 1 in.

No. 622

Dining or Library Table - $42.00

Height 30 in.
Length 84 in.
Width 42 in.
Thickness of Top 1⅝ in.

No. 624

Library Table - - - - - $38.00

Height 30 in.
Length 54 in.
Width 32 in.
Thickness of Top 1 in.

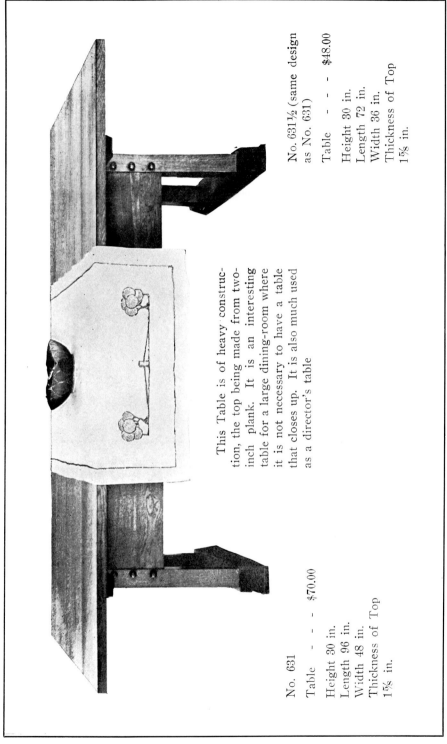

This Table is of heavy construction, the top being made from two-inch plank. It is an interesting table for a large dining-room where it is not necessary to have a table that closes up. It is also much used as a director's table

No. 631

Table - - - $70.00

Height 30 in.
Length 96 in.
Width 48 in.
Thickness of Top
1⅛ in.

No. 631½ (same design as No. 631)

Table - - - $48.00

Height 30 in.
Length 72 in.
Width 36 in.
Thickness of Top
1⅛ in.

No. 326

Arm Chair, Loose Seat
Cushion, Sheepskin - - - $15.00

Height of Back from Floor 37 in.
Height of Seat from Floor 18 in.
Size of Seat 19½ in. wide, 20½ in.
deep

No. 328

Dining Chair, Loose Seat
Cushion, Sheepskin - - - $10.00

Height of Back from Floor 37 in.
Height of Seat from Floor 18 in.
Size of Seat 19½ in. wide, 18 in. deep

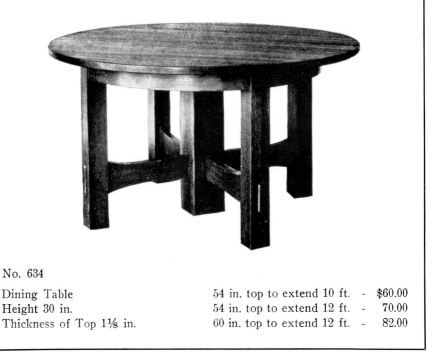

No. 634

Dining Table
Height 30 in.
Thickness of Top 1⅛ in.

54 in. top to extend 10 ft. -	$60.00
54 in. top to extend 12 ft. -	70.00
60 in. top to extend 12 ft. -	82.00

No. 817

Sideboard - - - - - - $84.00

Height to Top from Floor 41 in.
Height to Top of Plate Rail 50 in.
Length 70 in.

Depth 25 in.
Top Drawer lined with Ooze Leather

No. 354½

Dining Chair, Hard Leather
Seat - - - - - - - - $8.50

Height of Back from Floor 36 in.
Height of Seat from Floor 18 in.
Size of Seat 18 in. wide, 16 in. deep

No. 354½-A

Arm Chair, Hard Leather
Seat - - - - - - - - $12.50

Height of Back from Floor 36 in.
Height of Seat from Floor 18 in.
Size of Seat 20 in. wide, 18 in. deep

No. 815

China Cabinet - $45.00

Height 65 in.
Width 42 in.
Depth 15 in.
Three Stationary
Shelves on Line of
Mullions

No. 370-A

Arm Chair, Rush or
Soft Leather Slip
Seat - - - $11.00

Height of Back from
Floor 36 in.
Height of Seat from
Floor 18 in.
Size of Seat 20 in.
wide, 18 in. deep

No. 370

Occasional or
Side Chair,
Rush or Soft
Leather Slip
Seat - - $7.00

Height of Back
from Floor 36 in.
Height of Seat
from Floor 18 in.
Size of Seat 17
in. wide, 16 in.
deep

No. 814

Sideboard - - - - - - $68.00

Height to Top 38 in.
Height to Top of Plate Rail 49 in.
Width 66 in.
Depth 24 in.
Top Drawer lined with Ooze
Leather

No. 814½ (Same Design as No. 814)

Sideboard - - - - - - $50.00

Height to Top 38 in.
Height to Top of Plate Rail 49 in.
Width 56 in.
Depth 22 in.
Top Drawer lined with Ooze
Leather

No. 656
Dining Table
Height 30 in.
48 in. Top to extend
8 ft. - - - $48.00
54 in. Top to extend
10 ft. - - - $62.00
54 in. Top to extend
12 ft. - - - $72.00
60 in. Top to extend
12 ft. - - - $85.00
Thickness of Top
1⅛ in.

No. 816

Sideboard $34.00

Height to Top
38 in.
Height to Top
of Plate Rail
48 in.
Width 48 in.
Depth 18 in.
Top Small
Drawer Lined
with Ooze Leath-
er

No. 632

Dining Table
Height 30 in.

48 in. Top to Extend	8 ft.	$36.00
48 in. Top to Extend	10 ft.	41.00
54 in. Top to Extend	10 ft.	47.00
54 in. Top to Extend	12 ft.	53.00
60 in. Top to Extend	12 ft.	63.00

Thickness of Top 1 in.

No. 306½

Occasional or Dining Chair
Hard Leather Seat - - - $6.50

Height of Back from Floor 36 in.
Height of Seat from Floor 18 in.
Size of Seat 16 in. x 16 in.

No. 310½

Arm Chair, Hard Leather
Seat - - - - - - - - $10.50

Height of Back from Floor **36 in.**
Height of Seat from Floor 18 in.
Size of Seat 20 in. wide, 19 in. deep

No. 802

Serving Table - $18.00

Height 38 in.
Width 42 in.
Depth 18 in.

No. 818

Serving Table - $22.00

Height 39 in.
Width 48 in.
Depth 20 in.
Center Drawer lined
with Ooze Leather

No. 819

Sideboard - - $28.00

Height 39 in.
Length 48 in.
Depth 20 in.
Center Small Drawer
lined with Ooze
Leather

No. 820

China Cabinet - - $32.00

Height 60 in.
Width 36 in.
Depth 15 in.
Glass Sides
Stationary Shelves on Line
of Mullions

No. 353

Occasional or Side
Chair, Rush or Soft
Leather Slip Seat - $6.50

Height of Back from Floor
40 in.
Height of Seat from Floor
18 in.
Size of Seat 15 in. wide,
16 in. deep

No. 353-A

Arm Chair, Rush
or Soft Leather
Slip Seat $10.00

Height of Back
from Floor 41 in.
Height of Seat
from Floor 18 in.
Size of Seat 20
in. wide, 16 in.
deep

No. 841

Sideboard - - - - - - $175.00

Height to Top 38 in.
Height to Top of Back 42 in.

Width 72 in.
Depth 22 in.
Size of Cupboards 21 in. x 15 in.
Two small top Drawers lined
with Ooze Leather

No. 355

Dining Chair, Hard Leather Seat
and Back - - - - - $22.50

Height of Back from Floor 33 in.
Height of Seat from Floor 18 in.
Size of Seat 19 in. wide, 17 in.
deep

No. 355A

Arm Chair, Hard Leather Seat and
Back - - - - - - - $32.50

Height of Back from Floor 37 in.
Height of Seat from Floor 18 in.
Size of Seat 21 in. wide, 20 in.
deep

No. 840

Sideboard, with Glass - - - **$225.00**
Without Glass - - - - 190.00

Height to Top 40 in.
Height to Top of Mirror 60 in.
Width 84 in.
Depth 24 in.
Size of Glass 76 in. x 16 in.
Size of Cupboard 32 in. x 29 in.
Cupboard is fitted with a cedar tray
8 in. high.
Three top drawers on both sides are
lined with ooze leather

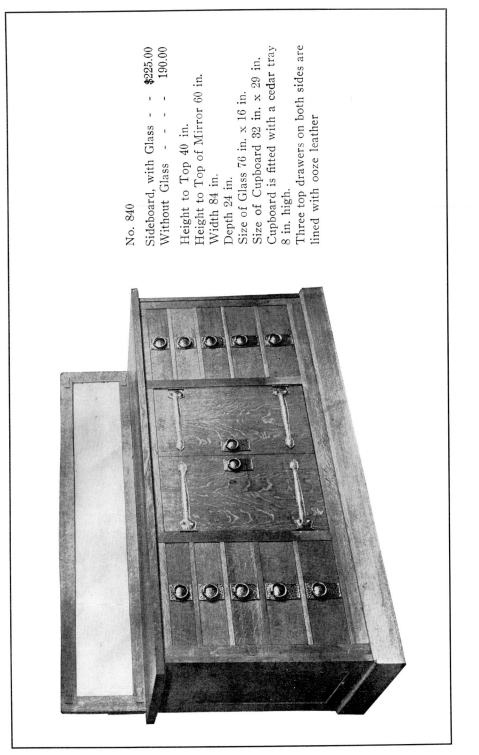

No. 349½

Chair, Hard Leather Seat - $8.00

Height of Back from Floor 38 in.
Height of Seat from Floor 18 in.
Size of Seat 18 in. wide, 16½ in.
deep

No. 349½-A

Arm Chair, Hard Leather
Seat - - - - - - - - $12.00

Height of Back from Floor 38 in.
Height of Seat from Floor 18 in.
Size of Seat 22 in. wide, 19 in. deep

No. 350

Occasional or Dining Chair,
Hard Leather Seat - - - $7.00

Height of Back from Floor 39 in.
Height of Seat from Floor 18 in.
Size of Seat 16 in. x 16 in.

No. 350-A

Arm Chair, Hard Leather
Seat - - - - - - - - $10.75

Height of Back from Floor 39 in.
Height of Seat from Floor 18 in.
Size of Seat 20 in. wide, 18 in. deep

No. 314

Arm Chair, Rush or Soft Leather
Slip Seat - - - - - - $9.00

Height of Back from Floor 40 in.
Height of Seat from Floor 18 in.
Size of Seat 21 in. wide, 18 in. deep
Seat tapered in Back to 19 in.

No. 308

Chair, Rush or Soft Leather Slip
Seat - - - - - - - $4.75

Height of Back from Floor 40 in.
Height of Seat from Floor 18 in.
Size of Seat 17 in. wide, 15 in. deep
Seat tapered in Back to 15 in.

No. 100

Umbrella Stand - - - $6.00

Height 24 in.
Diameter at Top 12 in.
Diameter at Base 9 in.
Wrought Iron Hoops
Copper Pan

No. 398

Desk Chair, Rush or Soft Leather
Slip Seat - - - - - - $4.50

Height of Back from Floor 32 in.
Height of Seat from Floor 18 in.
Size of Seat 17 in. wide, 15 in.
deep
Seat tapered in Back to 15 in.

No. 337

Sewing Rocker, Rush or Soft
Leather Slip Seat - - - - **$6.50**

Height of Back from Floor 35 in.
Height of Seat from Floor 14 in.
Size of Seat 16 in. wide, 15 in.
deep

No. 630

Sewing Table - - - - - **$18.50**
Height 28 in.
Top when closed 18 in. square
Top when opened 38 in. x 18 in.
Depth of top Drawer 4 in.
Depth of lower Drawer 6 in.
Top Drawer fitted with cedar
Tray

No. 308
Desk Chair, Rush
or Soft Leather Slip
Seat - - - **$4.75**
Height of Back
from Floor 40 in.
Height of Seat from
Floor 18 in.
Size of Seat 17 in.
wide, 15 in. deep
Seat tapered in
Back to 15 in.

No. 638
Drop-Leaf
Table - - $20.00
Height 29 in.
Top open 40 in. x
42 in.
Top closed 40 in.
x 14 in.

No. 92
Table
Cabinet - - $9.00
Height 9 in.
Length 24 in.
Depth 9 in.
Bottom covered
with Leather

No. 303

Rocker, Spring Seat Cushion,
Sheepskin - - - - - - $10.00
Height of Back from Floor 33 in.
Height of Seat from Floor 14 in.
Size of Seat 17 in. wide, 16 in.
deep

No. 387

Rocker, Spring Seat Cushion,
Sheepskin - - - - - - $10.50
Height of Back from Floor 42 in.
Height of Seat from Floor 15 in.
Size of Seat 17 in. wide, 18 in.
deep

No. 339

Arm Rocker, Rush or Soft Leather
Slip Seat - - - - - - $10.00
Height of Back from Floor 36 in.
Height of Seat from Floor 15 in.
Size of Seat 18 in. wide, 16 in.
deep

No. 340

Arm Chair, Rush or Soft Leather
Slip Seat - - - - - - $10.00
Height of Back from Floor 41 in.
Height of Seat from Floor 18 in.
Size of Seat 18 in. wide, 16 in.
deep

No. 912

Bed - - - - - - - - $30.00

Height of Head Board 51 in.
Height of Foot Board 45 in.
Length 75 in. (inside)
Width 54 in. (inside)

Also Made Single Size 40 in.
Wide - - - - - - - $26.00

Other Dimensions the Same

No. 914

Toilet Table - - - $26.00

Height to Top of Table 30 in.
Height to Top of Mirror
55 in.
Width 36 in.
Depth 18 in.
Glass 20 in. x 24 in.
Wood Knobs

No. 911

Dresser - - - $50.00

Height to Top of Dresser 33 in.
Height to Top of Mirror 66 in.
Width 48 in.
Depth 22 in.
Glass 28 in. x 34 in.
Wood Knobs
Ends Solid Panel

No. 913

Chest of Drawers $39.00

Height 51 in.
Width 36 in.
Depth 20 in.
Wood Knobs
Ends Solid Panel

No. 907

Dressing
Table $38.00

Height to Top 30 in.
Height to Top of Glass 54 in.
Length 48 in.
Depth 22 in.
Glass 38 in. x 20 in.

No. 906

Chest of Drawers $48.00

Height to Top 46 in.
Length 40 in.
Depth 20 in.

No. 905

Dresser - - - - - - - $65.00

Height to Top 33 in.
Height to Top of Glass 62 in.
Length 46 in.
Depth 22 in.
Glass 34 in. x 26 in.

No. 909

Chest of Drawers - - - $26.00

Height 42 in.
Width 36 in.
Depth 20 in.
Ends Paneled

No. 910

Mirror - - - - - - - $7.50

29 in. x 23 in.
Glass 26 in. x 20 in.
Chains and hooks included in above
price

No. 923

Bed, made in 3 Widths
all same Length 75 in.
(inside)
Width (inside) 36 in.
Head Board 46 in.
Foot Board 40 in. $16.00

Width (inside) 42 in.
Head Board 48 in.
Foot Board 42 in. $18.00

Width (inside) 54 in.
Head Board 50 in.
Foot Board 44 in. $20.00

No. 220

Couch Bed - - - - - - $24.00
Floss Mattress - - - - 12.50
Box Spring - - - - - 13.50
Complete, Including Floss
Mattress and Box Spring - $50.00
Height 34 in.
Width 36 in.
Length 84 in.
Craftsman Canvas Spread,
Embroidered, Extra - - - $8.00

Pillow Extra - - - - - $5.00

No. 641

Stand - - - - - $10.00

Height 29 in.
Width 20 in.
Depth 18 in.
Wood Knobs

No. 642

Stand - - - - - $12.00

Height 30 in.
Width 22 in.
Depth 17 in.
Wood Knobs

No. 922

Bed - - - - - - - - $36.00

Height of Head Board 54 in.
Height of Foot Board 45 in.
Length (inside) 75 in.
Width (inside) 54 in.

Single Size - - - - - - $30.00

Height of Head Board 50 in.
Height of Foot Board 42 in.
Length (inside) 75 in.
Width (inside) 40 in.

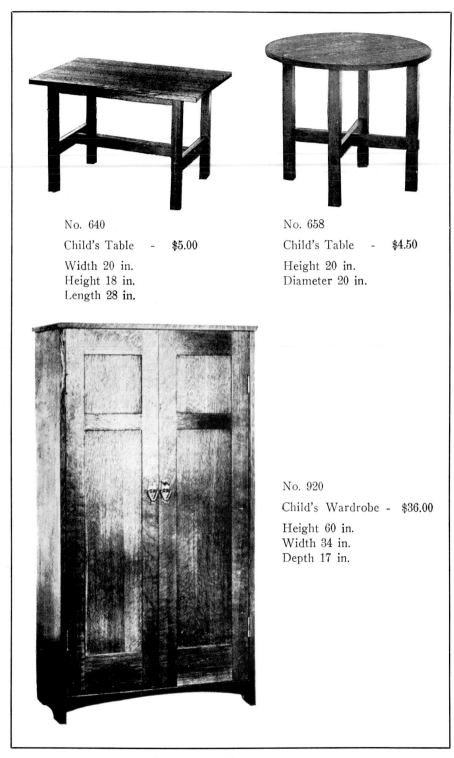

No. 640

Child's Table - $5.00

Width 20 in.
Height 18 in.
Length 28 in.

No. 658

Child's Table - $4.50

Height 20 in.
Diameter 20 in.

No. 920

Child's Wardrobe - $36.00

Height 60 in.
Width 34 in.
Depth 17 in.

No. 343

No. 344

Child's Arm Rocker - - - $4.50

Child's Arm Chair - - - $4.50

Height of Back from Floor 25 in.

Height of Back from Floor 26 in.
Height of Seat from Floor 11 in.
Size of Seat 15 in. wide, 12 in. deep

Height of Seat from Floor 11 in.
Size of Seat 15 in. wide, 12 in. deep
These Chairs Have Leather Seats

No. 920

Child's Wardrobe (open)

No. 341

Child's Rocker, Sheepskin - $3.25

Height of Back from Floor 23 in.
Height of Seat from Floor 11 in.
Size of Seat 13 in. wide, 12 in.
deep

No. 388

Child's High Chair - - - $9.00

Height of Back from Floor 42 in.
Height of Seat from Floor 24 in.
Size of Seat 15 in. wide, 12 in.
deep
Adjustable Tray
Rush Seat

No. 342

Child's Chair, Sheepskin - - $3.25

Height of Back from Floor 24 in.
Height of Seat from Floor 11 in.
Size of Seat 13 in. wide, 12 in.
deep

No. 211

Child's Settle - - - - - $8.00

Height of Back from Floor 31 in.
Height of Seat from Floor 13 in.
Width 42 in.
Depth 12 in.

No. 639

Child's Table - - - - - $8.00

Height 22½ in.
Length 36 in.
Width 22 in.
Thickness of Top ¾ in.

No. 919

Child's Bed - - - **$16**.00

Length 52 in. (inside)
Width 33 in. (inside)
Height of Ends 34 in.
Cane frame to hold mattress included in above price

No. 921

Child's Dresser - - $20.00

Height to Top of Dresser 29 in.
Height to Top of Mirror 49 in.
Width 36 in.
Depth 16 in.
Mirror 14 in. x 20 in.

No. 224

Hall Seat - - - - - - $32.00

Height of Back from Floor 42 in.
Height of Seat from Floor 17 in.
Length 48 in.
Depth 20 in.
The Seat Lifts forming a Box
which is 45 in. long x 8 in. deep

No. 216

Settle, Spring Seat Cushion
Soft Leather - - - - - $58.00

Height 29 in.
Length 79 in.
Width 31 in.

Sheepskin Pillows Extra, $8.00 each

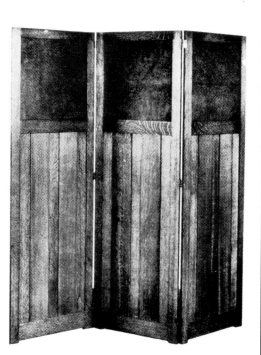

No. 91

Screen, Sheepskin
Panels - - - - $26.00

Height 68 in.
3 Panels, Width of Each
22 in.

No. 83

Screen,   Paneled
in Japanese Grass
Cloth   - - - $18.00

Paneled in Crafts-
man Canvas - $22.00

Height 66 in.
3 Panels, Width
of Each 22 in.

No. 68

Hall Mirror - - - - - $21.00

28 in. x 48 in.
End Glass 9 in. x 20 in.
Center Glass 20 in. x 20 in.
Iron Hooks

No. 67 (Same Design as No. 68)

Hall Mirror - - - - - $18.75

28 in. x 42 in.
End Glass 9 in. x 20 in.

No. 66

Hall Mirror - - - - - $16.00

28 in. x 36 in.
Glass 20 in. x 30 in.
Iron Hooks

Center Glass 16 in. x 20 in.
Iron Hooks
Chains and Hooks Included in Above Prices

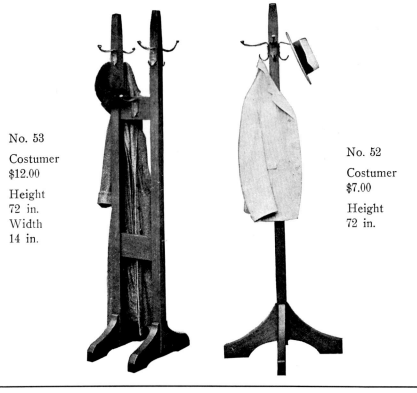

No. 53

Costumer
$12.00

Height
72 in.
Width
14 in.

No. 52

Costumer
$7.00

Height
72 in.

No. 54

Umbrella Stand   - - - - $5.00

Height 29 in.
12 in. square
Copper Pan

No. 55

Umbrella Stand   - - - - $7.00

Height 29 in.
Width 21 in.
Depth 12 in.
Copper Pan

No. 312½-B

Billiard Chair, Hard Leather
Seat - - - - - - - - $13.50

Height of Back from Floor 46 in.
Height of Seat from Floor 26 in.
Size of Seat 21 in. wide, 18 in. deep

No. 362

Desk Chair, Hard Leather
Seat - - - - - - - - $17.00

Height of Back from Seat 19 in.
Size of Seat 18 in. wide, 16 in. deep
Back Studded with Nails
Height Adjustable
Screw and Spring

CRAFTSMAN METAL WORK

IN the general review of Craftsman activities at the beginning of this book, I have already told why we were, in a manner, compelled to make metal trim for the furniture after our own designs and done in our own way. Having begun with the necessary drawer and door pulls, hinges and escutcheons, done from simple designs which were in harmony with the furniture, it was natural that we should go on with the making of other things along the same lines, as in the Craftsman scheme of interior decoration and furnishing there is a well-defined place for the right kind of metal work. In fact, the need for following out Craftsman designs in making all manner of household articles soon became as great as the original need for making furniture trim, for Craftsman fireplaces demanded Craftsman fire sets, hoods, andirons and coal buckets; and rooms finished with beams and wainscot in the Craftsman style needed the mellow glint of copper and brass here and there in lighting fixtures, lamps and the like. As the glittering lacquered surfaces and more or less fantastic designs of the machine-made fixtures were entirely out of harmony, we began to make lanterns of copper and brass after simple structural designs; electric and oil lamps of the same general character, and such articles as chafing dishes, trays, jardinières, umbrella stands and desk sets, our effort being all the time to keep to articles within the bounds of the useful, letting their decorative value grow out of their fitness for that use and the quality of the design and workmanship.

While most of our metal work is of the character already mentioned, we also do all kinds of architectural and decorative iron work, such as fireplace hoods and andirons of special design, hinges and door latches, window gratings, gates and doors, these being made to order and after designs furnished by the purchaser or made by ourselves at his request. We make rather a specialty of fireplace hoods and all manner of fireplace fittings. Also, we give special attention to designing lighting fixtures of all kinds to order, as we find that the purchaser frequently has a very clear idea of the kind of lamps, lanterns, etc., he would like to have in his home. When this is the case we make special designs to carry out ideas suggested to us, and have found this method so successful that we prefer to employ it whenever it is possible, as such special designs not only give more satisfaction to the person for whom they are made, but add greatly to our own range of ideas.

All of the articles indicated here, or illustrated and described in our metal catalogue, are made in iron, copper or brass, according to the metal needed to complete the color scheme of any given room. We also supply amateur cabinetmakers with the same metal trim which we use ourselves, so that when they make Craftsman furniture in their own workshops from designs which we furnish them, they need not be at a loss for the right metal trim.

This Desk Set, which contains nine pieces all made of hammered copper, is a luxurious equipment for a library table or a well-furnished office desk. The blotter pad is made of a large sheet of copper which projects slightly beyond the corners which hold the blotter. A sheet of felt covering the bottom prevents any danger of the metal marring the table. The pieces may all be had separately as follows:

Blotter Pad - - - - - - - - -	$5.00
Letter Holder - - - - - - - - -	3.75
Ink Well - - - - - - - - -	3.75
Stamp Box - - - - - - - - -	2.00
Hand Blotter - - - - - - - - -	1.25
Pen Tray - - - - - - - - -	1.25
Clip - - - - - - - - - - -	1.25
Letter Opener - - - - - - - -	1.25
Calendar - - - - - - - - - -	1.25
Desk Set, Complete 9 Pieces - - - -	20.00

No. 26
Vase of Hammered Copper or Brass - - - - - - - $4.50
Height 10½ in.
Diameter of Base 4 in.
Diameter at Top 6 in.

272   269

Ash Trays in Hammered Copper
No. 269. Diameter 4¾ in. - - - Price, 75c.
No. 272. Diameter 5½ in. - - - Price, 75c.

No. 369

Chafing Dish—Lid, Standard and Tray of Hammered Copper with Glazed Casserole

Price, with Tray - - $15.00

Capacity of Casserole 2 Quarts
Diameter of Tray 13 in.

Hammered Copper Nut Bowls,
Made in Three Sizes:

4 in. Diameter - - - - -	$1.75
5 in. Diameter - - - - -	2.25
6 in. Diameter - - - - -	3.75

Cider Set of Marblehead Pottery—

Pitcher and Six Mugs - - $11.00

With Copper Tray - - - - 15.00

Comes in a Deep Green or Old Blue

No. 233

Electric Candle Stick with Silk Shade in any desired color
$8.00

Candle Stick without Shade, not wired - - - $5.00
Height to Candle 9 in.
Diameter of Base 5 in.
Made in Hammered Copper or Brass

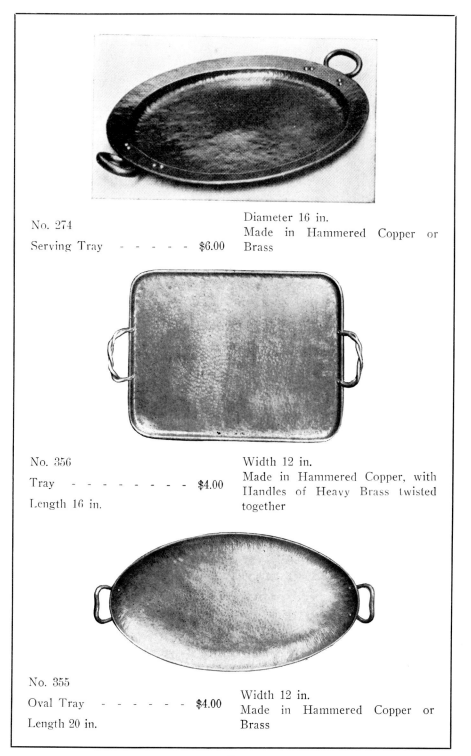

No. 274
Serving Tray - - - - - $6.00

Diameter 16 in.
Made in Hammered Copper or Brass

No. 356
Tray - - - - - - - - $4.00
Length 16 in.

Width 12 in.
Made in Hammered Copper, with Handles of Heavy Brass twisted together

No. 355
Oval Tray - - - - - $4.00
Length 20 in.

Width 12 in.
Made in Hammered Copper or Brass

No. 750

Dome, Panels of Amber
Tinted Hammered Glass,
framed in Copper - $40.00
Iron and Copper - 38.00
Iron - - - - - 35.00

Dome 6 in. deep, 20 in.
square, panels of amber
tinted hammered glass, 5
in. square, bound in metal,
swinging loose from rim.
Fitted for four electric
lights. Supplied complete
with chain and canopy

No. 760

Dome, Copper or Brass
Trim - - - - $78.00
Iron Trim - - - 75.00

Dome 8 in. deep, 24 in.
square, fumed oak frame
with mosaic favrile glass.
Swinging panels of amber
tinted hammered glass, 4¾
in. square, bound in metal.
Fitted for four electric
lights. Supplied complete
with chain and canopy

No. 730

Electrolier in Copper or
Brass - - - - - - - $40.00
In Iron and Copper - -   35.00
In Iron - - - - - -   33.00

Height of Lanterns 8 in.
Width of Lanterns 4 in.
Globe of Amber Tinted Ham-
mered Glass
Width of Crossbars, 17 in.
Supplied with Chain and Canopy

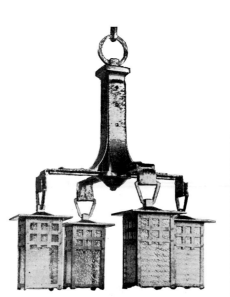

No. 764

Dome, in Copper or
Brass - - - - - - $90.00
In Iron - - - - -   87.00

Six amber tinted hammered
bent glass panels in dome,
with 18 small glass panels, 5
in. square, bound in metal,
swinging loose from the metal
rim of the dome
Diameter of Dome 26 in.
Fitted for four electric lights
Three candle brackets for use
in emergency
Supplied with Chain and
Canopy

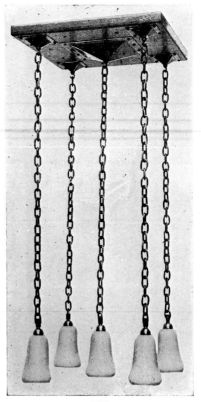

590

592

Nos. 590 and 592

Five-Light Electroliers, made with wrought iron chains, and canopies of hammered copper, brass, or iron attached to a ceiling plate of fumed oak. Bell-shaped globes in crystal, amber or straw-colored opalescent glass. Also made with lanterns

Nos. 591 and 593

Nine-Light Electrolier (Same Design as No. 590)

In Copper or Brass, with Bells - - - - - - - -	$38.00
In Iron, with Bells - - -	35.00
In Copper or Brass, with Lanterns - - - - - -	56.00
In Iron, with Lanterns - -	52.00

In Copper or Brass, with Bells - - - - - - - -	$22.00
In Iron, with Bells - - -	20.00
In Copper or Brass, with Lanterns (same as used on No. 733, page 89) - -	30.00
In Iron, with Lanterns - -	26.50

The only difference between these lights is in the shape of the ceiling plate. Nos. 590 and 591 have the round plate, while in Nos. 592 and 593 the plate is square

No. 733

Five-Light Electrolier,
in Copper or Brass - $50.00
Iron and Copper - - 48.00
Iron - - - - - - 45.00

Diameter of Band 26 in.
Width of Band 4 in.
Height of Lanterns 10 in.
Diameter of Lanterns 4 in.
Lanterns furnished with Opalescent, Crystal or Amber Glass.
Supplied with Chain and Canopy

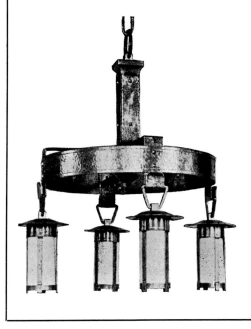

No. 731

Electrolier, in Copper or
Brass - - - - - - $35.00
Iron and Copper - - 32.00
Iron - - - - - - 30.00

Diameter of Band 20 in.
Width of Band 3 in.
Height of Lanterns 8 in.
Diameter of Lanterns 3½ in.
Lanterns furnished with Opalescent, Crystal or Amber Glass.
Supplied with Chain and Canopy

No. 702

Newel Post Lamp, in Copper
or Brass - - - - - - $12.00
Iron - - - - - - - -   10.50

Height of Lantern 8 in.
Base 4 in. square
Amber tinted hammered Glass

No. 203

Electric Lantern for hall
or porch, complete with
canopy of same metal as
lantern, and chain of
wrought iron
Copper or Brass - $30.00
Iron - - - - -   24.50

Height 20 in.
Roof 14 in. square
Base 9 in. square
Amber tinted hammered
Glass

No. 203½ (Same Design as No. 203)

Electric Lantern, complete with
canopy of same metal as lantern,
chain of wrought iron
Copper or Brass - - - - $24.00

Iron - - - - - - - - - $21.00

Height 12 in.
Roof 11 in. square
Base 7 in. square
Amber tinted hammered Glass

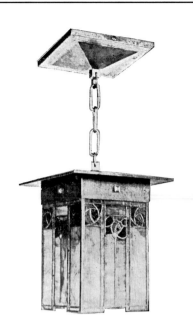

No. 777

Electric Lantern, complete with
canopy and chain of same metal
as lantern, in Copper or
Brass - - - - - - - - $25.00

Height of Lantern 14 in.
Base 7 in. square
Mosaic Favrile Glass Panels

No. 766

Electric Lantern, complete with
canopy of same metal as lantern,
and chain of wrought iron, in
Copper or Brass - - - - $18.00
Iron - - - - - - - - 16.00

Height of Lantern 16 in.
12 in. square
Amber Tinted Antique Glass
Fitted with Glass Door at bottom

No. 515
Electric Lantern, Complete with
Canopy of same Metal as Lantern
and Chain of Wrought Iron
Copper or Brass - - - - $11.00
Iron - - - - - - - - 9.00
Height 9½ in.
Top 6½ in. Square
Base 5 in. Square
Amber Tinted Hammered Glass
Fitted with Glass Door at Bottom

No. 509
Electric Lantern with Bracket
Copper or Brass - - - - $8.00
Iron - - - - - - - - 7.00
Height of Bracket 10 in.
Projection of Bracket 7 in.
Height of Lantern 7 in.
Base 4½ in. Square
Panels of Amber Tinted Hammered
Glass, 4½ in. Square, bound in
Metal, swinging loose from Rim

No. 304
Electric Lantern with Bracket
Copper or Brass - - - - $10.00
Iron - - - - - - 8.00
Diameter of Canopy 5 in.
Projection of Bracket 6 in.
Height of Lantern 10 in.
Diameter of Lantern at Base 4 in.
Globe of Crystal, Amber or Straw
Colored Opalescent Glass

No. 305
Electric Lantern with Bracket
(same design as No. 304)
Copper or Brass - - - - $8.00
Iron - - - - - - - 7.00
Diameter of Canopy 5 in.
Projection of Bracket 6 in.
Height of Lantern 8 in.
Diameter at Base 3 in.

No. 228

Electric Side Light with Two Lanterns
Copper or Brass - $14.00
Iron   - - - -   11.50

Size of Wall Canopy
5½ in. Square
Projection of Arms 12 in.
Spread of Arms 12 in.
Height of Lantern 8 in.
Diameter of Lantern at Base 3 in.
Globe of Crystal, Amber or Straw Colored Opalescent Glass

No. 400

Bell Light with Bracket
Copper or Brass - - - - $4.50
Iron - - - - - - - -   3.75

Bell Shaped Globe of Crystal, Amber or Straw colored Opalescent Glass
Height of Globe 6½ in.
Diameter 4¾ in.
Height of Bracket 10 in.
Projection 8 in.

No. 513

Electric Sconce, Complete with Mica Shade
Copper or Brass - - - - $8.00
Iron - - - - - - - -   7.50

Height of Sconce 12 in.
Width of Sconce 6 in.
Projection of Bracket 5 in.
Base of Shade 4 in.

No. 512

Electric Sconce (same design and size as No. 513, but fitted with two lights)
Copper or Brass - - - - $12.00
Iron - - - - - - - -   11.00

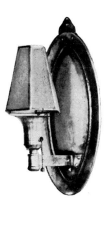

No. 506

Electric Lamp - - - $12.00

Height 16½ in.
Length 10½ in.
Width at the Base 9 in.
The Shade is made of glass set in a copper frame and may be tilted to reveal or shade the light as desired. Two thicknesses of glass are used, the outer layer being hammered antique glass in green or amber and the inner more in the nature of porcelain. Fitted for one electric bulb.

No. 506

No. 502
Electric Lamp
With Glass Shade - - - $15.00
With Sweet Grass Shade - 7.50
Height 17 in.
Base 7 in. x 7 in.
Diameter of Shade 12 in.
Stand made of wood banded with copper at the top and bottom of the shaft. The shade is made of small panes of opalescent glass set in copper

No. 502

No. 504

Electric Lamp with Shade of Japanese Wicker - - - - $12.00

Height 20 in.
Base 7½ in. x 7½ in.
Diameter of shade 17 in.
Fitted for Three Electric Bulbs

No. 504

No. 262

Electric Lamp in Copper with Shade of Opalescent Glass and Copper Bands
Lamp Complete with Shade - $32.00
Price of Shade - - - - 10.00

Height of Lamp over all 22 in.
Diameter of Base 7 in.
Diameter of Shade 16 in.
Fitted for Three Electric Bulbs

No. 262

No. 625

No. 625

Electric Lamp of Fumed Oak and Hammered Copper, Complete with Shade of Hammered Copper Cut into Fretwork Panels and Lined with Opalescent Glass - - - - - - - $40.00
Complete with Shade of Japanese Wicker - - - $20.00

Octagonal Shaft and Base Made of Fumed Oak, Bands and Shade Support of Copper
Height to Saucer 16½ in
Base 10½ in.
Diameter of Shade 18 in.
Fitted for Three Electric Bulbs

No. 139

Fire Set, consisting of wall bracket, shovel, poker and tongs, all in wrought iron

Set Complete - - - - - $18.00
Wall Bracket - - - - - 3.50
Shovel - - - - - - - - 5.00
Tongs - - - - - - - - 6.00
Poker - - - - - - - - 3.50

Height of each Piece 48 in.
Width of Bracket 2 in.
Thickness of Bracket ⅜ in.
Spread of Bracket 14 in.

No. 348

Andirons. Made in Wrought
Iron - - - - - - - - $24.00
Height 28 in.
Depth 26 in.

CRAFTSMAN FABRICS & NEEDLEWORK

THE fabrics chosen for window curtains, table scarfs, squares, center-pieces, pillow covers, and other draperies and small furnishings of a room, form an important part of the decorative scheme. When the color, texture and decoration of these harmonize with the color and character of the woodwork, the finish of the wall surface and the kind of furniture used, the result is entirely harmonious and restful, but an error in any one of these particulars is sufficient to ruin a whole scheme of decoration that is otherwise pleasant and satisfying. Therefore, we give special attention to fabrics and needlework, because the Craftsman room is so strongly individual that a jarring note in any of its minor furnishings is perceived at once. We are constantly searching for fabrics of interesting color and weave, and we have been so far successful that we are able to carry a large stock of materials, ranging in weight from heavy canvas for pillows and portières to sheer, loosely woven net for window curtains. We also do a great deal of needlework in bold, simple designs. using the outline stitch, the simple darning stitch and appliqué to get the broader decorative effects we desire. To those of our patrons who like to do such needlework at home we send on request prices of materials stamped with any design selected and sufficient floss for working. We are also glad to send samples of our fabrics to all who wish to purchase.

CRAFTSMAN CANVAS

ONE of the most satisfying of our materials for portières, pillow covers, upholstery—in fact, for any use where a rugged effect is desired—is Craftsman Canvas. This is woven of jute and flax and is dyed in the piece, the different threads taking the dye in a way that causes an interesting variation in tone. The canvas comes in three tones of wood brown, one with a cool grayish look in which there is a suggestion of green; another with a sunny, yellowish tone; and the third with enough red in it to make it almost a dark russet. Among the reds there are rust color, brick red, old rose and bright deep crimson. The greens have the foliage hues, shading from a brownish green like rusty pine needles, through the leaf and grass green shades up to a very gray green with a bluish tinge like a eucalyptus leaf. The blues are in the ocean tones, and there are three tones of yellow, ranging from wheat color to golden brown. The best decorative effects are obtained on this material by designs in appliqué, with heavy couched outlines, but it is also effective when ornamented with drawn work, darned work, quaint patterns in cross stitch and bold embroidery in linen floss.

Craftsman Canvas, 50 inches wide, price per yard, $1.25.

ANTIQUE LINEN

THIS material is particularly good for fairly heavy window curtains where it is necessary to give a warm tint to the light admitted into the room. The weave is loose and coarse and the thread loosely twisted and irregular, giving not only an unusually interesting texture, but also a quality of translucency that produces a richer and deeper tone of color when the light shines through it than appears in the piece. The color that we find best for curtains is a rather deep straw, that takes on almost an apricot tone when the light shines through it, giving the effect of a glow of sunlight in the room. This canvas comes also in soft olive green and in a vivid green like the color of young grass, both of which are charming for upholstery and chair cushions, especially when used with the willow furniture and in connection with distinctly summer furnishings. Another color is a dull golden brown, which is desirable not only for upholstery, but also for table squares, scarfs, etc., as it blends admirably with the tone of fumed oak.

Antique Linen, 36 inches wide, price per yard, 85 cents.

HAND-WOVEN LINEN

THIS is a material like crash, rough in texture, irregular in weave and comes in the natural color. It is woven only fifteen inches wide, which is just the right width for buffet and dresser scarfs and table runners, but not wide enough for squares and centerpieces. While, like the other materials, it makes a good ground for appliqué or darned work, we find that the all-white embroidery, in which the designs are worked in satin stitch with pure white linen floss, is especially effective upon its rough gray surface.

Hand-woven Linen, 15 inches wide, price per yard, 25 cents.

FLEMISH LINEN

FLEMISH Linen has a fine close weave, and is very effective for scarfs, centerpieces and the like. It is woven with a round thread, which gives to the fabric a matt finish and makes it very soft and pliable to the touch. This linen comes in three shades, white, ecru and brownish gray. It furnishes a delightful background for designs in embroidery or appliqué when carried out in the more delicate tones, and is a most desirable fabric for luncheon sets, table napkins and napery of all kinds. The soft texture and matt surface of this linen make it much more sympathetic to the touch than damask, and its color blends beautifully with the wood of an oak table.

Flemish Linen, 50 inches wide, price per yard, $1.00.

CRAFTSMAN CASEMENT LINEN

W E HAVE no more desirable material than this for window curtains, because it is one of the few we know that looks better when the light shines through it than it does against an opaque surface or in the piece. It is a loosely woven linen of about the weight and weave of rough Shantung silk, and against the light shows a delightfully irregular thread. This fabric is admirably adapted to darned work or stenciling in contrasting colors, as it has sufficient body to allow the colors to show even against the light. The material comes in plain linen in the natural creamy gray tones.

Craftsman Casement Linen, 36 inches wide, price per yard, 35 cents.

CRAFTSMAN CURTAIN NETS

T HESE are the best materials we know for sheer window curtains which are meant to admit the light freely and yet to mellow and temper it as it enters the room. We carry three of these nets, which all come in the natural linen color. One is a plain, square-meshed net, very loosely woven, soft and flexible. Then we have a net of about the same weight, but woven so that it is like lattice work, and another latticed net that is very much heavier, the meshes being as thick as twine, but flat and very soft. This net is specially desirable for bold effects, as it shows strong opaque lines and blocks against the light, instead of being translucent as are the lighter nets.

Plain Curtain Net, 42 inches wide, price per yard, 70 cents.
Light Lattice Net, 48 inches wide, price per yard, 75 cents.
Heavy Lattice Net, 48 inches wide, price per yard, $1.75.

LINSELL CASEMENT FABRIC

L INSELL is a sheer, loosely woven fabric made of pure linen threads. We carry it in two weights, one as fine and thin as scrim and the other woven quite as loosely, but of heavier thread. This fabric admits the light freely, as the heavier weight is of such open weave that it is as translucent as the other. The finer woven quality comes in tea color, light wood brown, delft blue and leaf green, and the heavier weave in straw color, coffee color, copper color and wood brown.

Linsell, both weaves 36 inches wide, price per yard, 75 cents.

CRAFTSMAN CURTAIN SCRIM

T HE character of this fabric is well known. We carry an especially firm and well-woven scrim, plain, cross-barred and figured, in white and cream. The figured scrim is cream color, with small conventionalized flowers embroidered in leaf green and apricot yellow, or green and rose.

Plain and Cross-barred Scrim, 36 inches wide, price per yard, 35 cents.
Figured Scrim, 65 inches wide, price per yard, $1.25. 52 inches wide, price per yard, 65 cents.

Table Scarf of Craftsman Canvas, Horse Chestnut Design in appliqué upon dull olive green canvas with a band of bloom linen in pale rose and green. The trees are done in brownish yellow floss, and the nuts in old rose

Craftsman Canvas, complete, 20 in. x 72 in. - $4.00
20 in. x 90 in. - 4.50
Flemish Linen, complete
20 in. x 72 in. - - - $3.75
20 in. x 90 in. - - - 4.25

Portière of Craftsman Canvas, Horse Chestnut Design. Made of dark leaf green canvas with an applied band of linen in a much lighter shade of the same green. The tree trunks, branches and outlines are done in soft wood brown floss, and the nuts are embroidered in peach colored floss

9 ft. long, 4 ft. wide, per Pair - - - $19.00
Stamped Canvas with all materials for working - - - - - $12.00

Pillow. Pine Cone Design. Done in appliqué of dull brown Craftsman Canvas against Craftsman Canvas of a soft, dull corn color with the pine needles outlined in soft green floss

Pillow Complete 25 in. x 25 in. - - - - - - $5.00
Pillow Cover Complete - 3.50
Stamped Canvas and Material for Working - - - - 1.75

Portière. Pine Cone Design. Done in appliqué upon gray-green Craftsman canvas. The broad band is of oak brown canvas applied with couching of the same color. The applied pine cones are of dull brown linen very like the real cones, and the pine needles are outlined in floss of a darker shade than the cones

9 ft. long, 4 ft. wide, per Pair - - - - - - $18.00
Stamped Canvas with all materials for working - $12.00

Table Scarf. Ginkgo Design. Done in appliqué on Flemish linen. This design is frequently done in deep leaf green linen appliqué, outlined and couched in rich cream color with the buds on the upright stalks done in brilliant orange

Craftsman Canvas complete,
20 in. x 72 in. - - - $4.25
20 in. x 90 in. - - - 4.75
Flemish Linen complete,
20 in. x 72 in. - - - $4.00
20 in. x 90 in. - - - 4.50

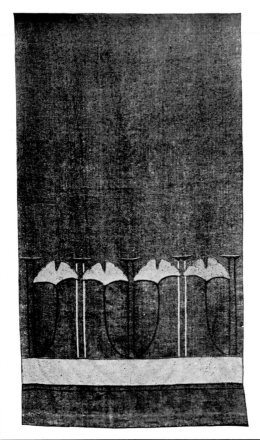

Portière. Ginkgo Design. Done in appliqué upon Craftsman Canvas. As shown here, the portière is of olive brown canvas with the applied leaves and broad band of russet bloom linen, and the stems and couching of soft wood brown linen floss. The tall, straight stems are done in floss of the natural flax color with tips of brilliant orange

9 ft. Long, 4 ft. Wide, per pair - - - - - - $20.00
Stamped Canvas with all materials for working - $13.00

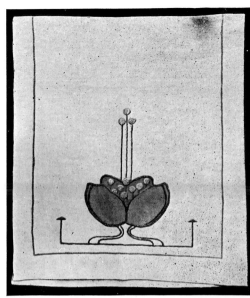

Table Scarf. Lotus Design in appliqué. Done upon natural - colored Flemish linen with an applied design in dull rose linen, embroidered and couched with floss of light olive green, and seeds of clear gold color

Craftsman Canvas complete
20 in. x 72 in. - - $4.35
20 in. x 90 in. - - 4.85
Flemish Linen complete,
20 in. x 72 in. - $4.10
20 in. x 90 in. - - 4.60

Portière. Seed Pod Design. Done on yellow brown Craftsman canvas with the applied seed pods in rusty green canvas, outlined with a couching of brown floss, the same shade as the background. The seeds and the tall straight stems branching out at the top are of the same brown, and the twisted trailing stems are outlined in rusty green like the pods. The bright band at the bottom is of the same canvas as the pods, outlined with brown

9 ft. Long, 4 ft. Wide, price per Pair - - - - - $20.00
Stamped Canvas with all materials for working - $13.00

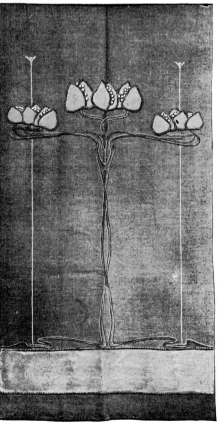

Curtain. Conventionalized Wild Rose Design. Done on wood brown linsell. The applied bands of linen are exactly the same color as the curtain, and are couched down with strands of darker brown linen floss. The petals are outlined with brown floss, and the central dots are in burnt orange and dark wood brown

Curtains complete, per pair
2¼ or 2 Yds. Long - $10.00
1½ Yds. Long - - 9.00

Portière. Conventionalized Wild Rose Design. Done on Craftsman canvas of a dark gray blue tone. The applied band is of bloom linen in changing tones of pale blue and green, and the couching is done in linen floss of a burnt straw color in which there is a decided greenish cast. The embroidered dots are in this same straw color and in bright coral

9 ft. Long, 4 ft. Wide, per Pair
$18.00
Stamped Canvas with all Materials for Working - - - $13.00

Couch Cover. Done on Craftsman canvas with poppy design and broad band in linen appliqué. As illustrated here the applied leaves are of golden bloom linen, and the couching and stems of soft medium brown upon a dull brownish yellow canvas

Couch Cover complete made in any size desired - - - - - $17.00
Stamped Canvas with all materials for working - - - - - $13.00

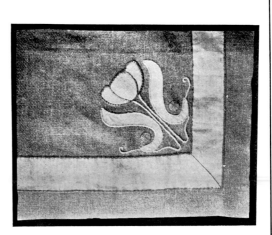

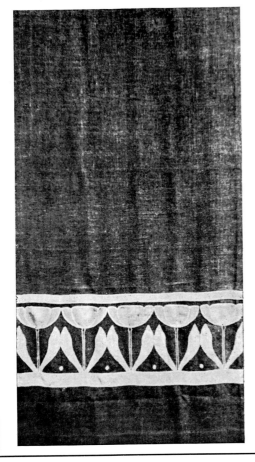

Portière. Poppy Design. Done on grayish green Craftsman canvas. The blossoms and lower band are of golden bloom linen, and the leaves and upper band are of linen in a pale shade of leaf green. The couchings and outlines are done in golden brown floss, and the needed color accent is given by the small dots of deep vivid red. Like all the Craftsman draperies, this portière is made up in any color scheme desired.

9 ft. long, 4 ft. wide, per pair - - - - - - $20.00
Stamped Canvas with all materials for working - $13.00

Table Scarf. Pomegranate Design. Done on wood brown Craftsman canvas with appliqué in golden yellow bloom linen, seeds and outlines in gray green floss, and the couching in old gold floss. This design is also carried out on Flemish linen, with appliqué of yellow bloom linen, seeds of deep rosy red, and couching and outlines in leaf green

Craftsman Canvas, complete		Flemish Linen, complete	
12 in. x 12 in. - - - - -	$2.00	12 in. x 12 in. - - - - -	$1.90
22 in. x 22 in. - - - - -	3.75	22 in. x 22 in. - - - - -	3.60
24 in. x 24 in. - - - - -	4.25	24 in. x 24 in. - - - - -	4.15
26 in. x 26 in. - - - - -	4.75	26 in. x 26 in. - - - - -	4.60

Table Square. Seed pod design carried out on Craftsman canvas or Flemish linen. As shown here, the linen is used with appliqué of soft olive green linen, outlines and couching of golden brown floss, and seeds of deep orange. The same design is frequently done on Craftsman canvas in rich dark colors for library tables and the like

Craftsman Canvas, complete
12 in. x 12 in. - - - -	$2.00
22 in. x 22 in. - - - -	3.75
24 in. x 24 in. - - - -	4.25
26 in. x 26 in. - - - -	4.75

Flemish Linen, complete
12 in. x 12 in. - - - -	$1.90
22 in. x 22 in. - - - -	3.60
24 in. x 24 in. - - - -	4.15
26 in. x 26 in. - - - -	4.60

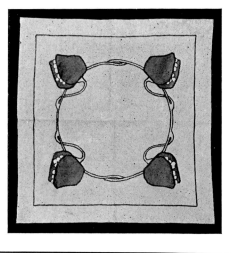

Pillow. Orange Design. Done on warm reddish brown Craftsman canvas with appliqué of golden bloom linen outlined with olive floss. Another effective combination is carried out on dull yellow canvas with appliqué in a clear light orange tone, and outlines in soft brown

Pillow complete, 25 in. x 25 in. - - - - - - $5.00
Pillow Cover complete 3.50
Stamped Canvas and materials for working - 1.75

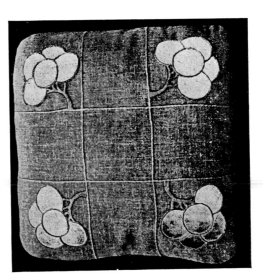

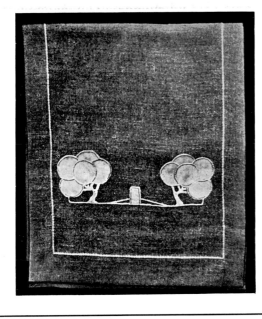

Table Scarf. Orange design on copper-colored Craftsman canvas with appliqué of russet bloom outlined in wood brown floss. Accent is given by a touch of black at either side of the small center square

Craftsman Canvas, complete
20 in. x 72 in. - - $4.00
20 in. x 90 in. - - 4.50

Flemish Linen, complete
20 in x 72 in. - - $3.75
20 in. x 90 in. - - 4.25

Table Scarf. China Tree Design. Done on hand-woven linen. The design is darned in light leaf green linen floss, the threads running straight across with the woof. The outlines of trees and branches are afterwards picked out with a broken thread of dark blue, run in stitches of short uneven lengths around the edges

Hand-Woven Linen Scarf, complete
15 in. x 72 in. - - - $2.00
15 in. x 90 in. - - -   2.50

Dresser or Sideboard Scarf. Umbel Design. Done on Flemish linen. The design is carried out entirely in satin stitch with pure white linen floss, giving the effect of solid white decoration against the natural gray of the linen. These scarfs serve equally well as table runners

Flemish Linen Scarf, complete,
20 in. x 72 in. - - - $5.00
20 in. x 90 in. - - -   5.50
20 in. x 99 in. - - -   5.75

Scarf for Bureau or Dressing Table. Zinnia Design. Done on heavy gray linen which has a natural colored warp and a pure white woof, giving it a peculiar silvery shimmer. The design is darned and outlined in pure white linen floss.

Heavy Gray Linen, complete
20 in. x 72 in. - - - $5.25
20 in. x 90 in. - - - 5.50

Linen Stamped with all materials for Working
20 in. x 72 in. - - - $2.75
20 in. x 90 in. - - - 2.50

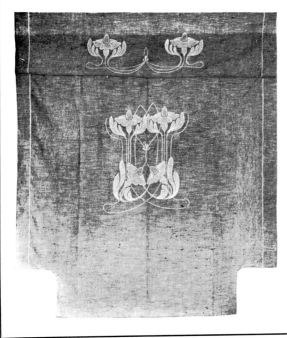

Bedspread. Zinnia design in all white embroidery. Done on heavy gray linen like that described above.

Complete - - - $20.00

Linen stamped with all materials for Working,
$14.00

This linen comes 72 in. wide and therefore is most satisfactory for bedspreads, as there are no seams necessary.

Linen 72 in. wide, price per Yard - - - $1.75

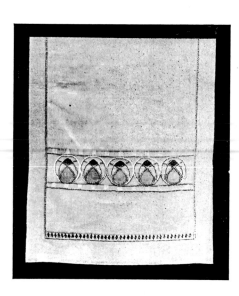

Table Scarf. Crocus Design. Done on Craftsman canvas or Flemish linen. As illustrated here, the appliqué is of blue and green bloom linen, and the couching and outlining in various shades of bright blue upon a scarf of natural-colored linen. This design is also very effective when the same colors are used upon Craftsman canvas of a deep gray blue. A sharp accent is given by the use of a spot of gleaming orange just above each piece of appliqué

Craftsman Canvas, complete
20 in. x 72 in. - - - - $4.00
20 in. x 90 in. - - - - 4.90

Flemish Linen, complete
20 in. x 72 in.   - - - $3.75
20 in. x 90 in.   - - - 4.25

Round Table Cover. Pomegranate Design. This is made for a large round or octagonal table such as would be used in the library or living room. It is made in any color scheme desired, but we have found that one of the most satisfactory is done on dark blue Craftsman linen with the couched lines in wood brown and the berries in bright orange

Complete on Craftsman linen, 48 in. in diameter, $7.00

Stamped linen and all materials for working - $4.00

Table Cover. Magnolia Design. Done on hand-woven linen of a creamy gray color. The leaves and flowers of the pattern are done in darned work, and the design is worked out in four colors, the blossoms in clear dark red, the stamens in burnt orange, and the leaves in dull green with outlines in green and gray brown

Complete
44 in. x 44 in. - - $9.00
36 in. x 36 in. - - 7.50

Sideboard or Table Scarf. Magnolia Design. Done on hand-woven linen to match the table cover or in any color combination desired.

Complete
20 in. x 90 in. - - $5.50

Table Scarf. Dragon Fly Design. Done on hand-woven linen in colors like those of old Persian embroidery, the principal tones being green, blue and old rose

Complete in Hand-Woven Linen
15 in. x 72 in. - - - $2.00
15 in. x 90 in. - - - 2.50

Table Scarf. Dogwood Design. Done on hand-woven linen with a background darned in white floss. The petals are outlined in dark blue, and the flower centers are done in French knots of the same color
Complete in Hand - Woven Linen

15 in. x 72 in. - - - $2.00
15 in. x 90 in. - - - 2.50

Table Scarf. Pine Cone Design in darned work, on hand-woven linen, the cones done in brown and the border lines and upright dividing lines in dull rusty green.

Complete in Hand-Woven Linen

15 in. x 72 in. - - - $2.00
15 in. x 90 in. - - - 2.50

Curtain. Pine Cone Design. Done in darning stitch on casement linen of a natural brownish tone. The design is carried out in sage green and golden brown

Curtain Fretwork Design on casement linen. The geometrical figure of the design is done mainly in bright golden brown outlined with silvery sage green, with a figure in the center of each square done in pale coral

Price for above curtains complete
2¼ or 2 Yds. Long - $8.00
1½ Yds. Long - - 7.50

These curtains are also very beautiful when decorated simply with a border in drawn work—a method of ornamentation to which the weave is admirably adapted. The prices for curtains of this material bordered with drawn work down the side and across the bottom are:
2¼ or 2 Yds. Long - $6.00
1½ Yds. Long - - 5.25

Curtain. Made of casement linen in the natural brownish tone, with a band of two-toned bloom linen and outlines of linen floss

Complete
2¼ or 2 Yds. Long - $7.00
1½ Yds. Long - - 6.50

Craftsman Net Curtain in pattern No. 3. Made of square-meshed net in natural line color with borders done in darning stitch with white or cream colored linen floss

Complete, per pair,
2¼ Yds. Long - - $10.00
2 Yds. Long - - 9.00
1½ Yds. Long - - 7.75

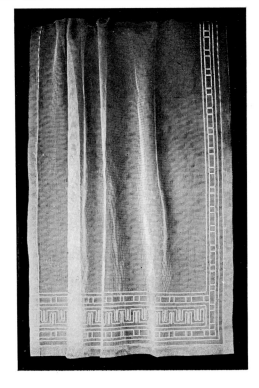

Craftsman Net Curtain in pattern No. 1, showing wide band across the bottom and narrow border up the side. Done in darning stitch with linen floss in the same combination of colors described above

Complete, per pair
2¼ Yds. Long - - - $8.50
2 Yds. Long - - - 7.75
1½ Yds. Long - - - 6.75

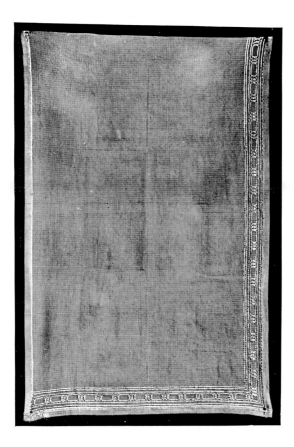

Craftsman Net Curtain in pattern No. 7, with very simple border. Done in darning stitch in the color combination already described

Complete, per pair
2¼ Yds. Long - - - - $7.50
2   Yds. Long - - - - 7.00
1½ Yds. Long - - - - 6.50

To those who wish to make their own curtains we will be glad to send any quantity of net desired, together with floss sufficient for working and a pattern showing the design selected

Craftsman Curtain Net
42 in. Wide, per Yard - - $0.70
Floss per skein - - - - - .05

CRAFTSMAN WILLOW FURNITURE

The right kind of willow furniture affords so exactly the relief that is necessary to lighten the general effect of the darker and heavier oak pieces that we have come to believe that a room to be satisfactorily furnished should have one or two pieces. Especially is it desirable in combination with our heavier oak furniture, as it is as simple in line and natural in finish as the more severe and massive oaken chairs and settles. All these chairs, while strongly and firmly made, have yet the flexibility of a well-woven basket

We finish these willow chairs in two colors, a soft green and deep golden brown. In both cases the color is more or less uneven, varying as it might in the branches themselves

The cushions are covered with Craftsman canvas, but of course these coverings either in color or materials could be varied to suit any scheme of furnishing. For a summer cottage or bungalow a chintz or cretonne is particularly attractive for the cushion coverings. The prices quoted include cushions

No. 70

Settle, including two Pillows $68.00

Height of Back from floor 32 in.
Height of Seat from floor 17 in.
Length over all 86 in.
Size of Seat 78 in. long x 27 in. deep

No. 72

Willow Settle - - - - - $43.00

Height of Back from Floor 33 in.
Height of Arm from Floor 28 in.

Height of Seat from Floor 17 in.
Length over all 66 in.
Size of Seat 54 in. long x 26 in. deep

No. 60

Willow Chair - - - - - $24.50

Height of Back from Floor 39 in.

Height of Arm from Floor 30 in.
Height of Seat from Floor 17 in.
Size of Seat 22 in. wide x 23 in. deep

No. 56

Willow Chair - - $20.00

Height of Arm from Floor
31 in.
Height of Seat from Floor
17 in.
Size of Seat 22 in. wide x
23 in. deep

No. 50

Willow Chair - - - - - $20.00

Height of Back from Floor 34 in.
Height of Seat from Floor 15 in.
Size of Seat 21 in. wide x 19 in.
deep

No. 54

Willow Chair - - - - - $12.00

Height of Back from Floor 33 in.
Height of Seat from Floor 17 in.
Size of Seat 20 in. wide x 19 in.
deep.

No. 64

Willow Chair - - - - - $22.50

Height of Back from Floor 33 in.
Height of Arm from Floor 28 in.
Height of Seat from Floor 17 in.
Size of Seat 21 in. wide x 23 in.
deep

No. 82

Willow Chair - - - $18.00

Height of Back from Floor 41 in.

Height of Seat from Floor 17 in.

Size of Seat 20 in. wide x 18 in. deep

No. 83

Willow Rocker - - $18.00

(Same design and dimensions as No. 82)

No. 54½

Willow Chair - - - $14.00

Height of Back from Floor 33 in.

Height of Seat from Floor 17 in.

Size of Seat 20 in. wide x 19 in. deep

No. 58

Willow Arm Chair - $17.00

Height of Back from Floor
37 in

Height of Seat from Floor
15 in.

Size of Seat 21 in. wide x 19
in. deep

No. 59

Willow Arm Rocker, $17.00

(Same design and dimensions as No. 58)

No. 68

Willow Chair - - - $10.00

Height of Back from Floor
37 in.

Height of Seat from Floor
17 in.

Size of Seat 21 in. wide x 20
in. deep

CRAFTSMAN RUGS

We have taken great pains to find the kind of rug that will harmonize in character as well as in color with the complete scheme of Craftsman furnishing. To be in keeping with the general idea of a Craftsman room, a rug should be apparently, as well as actually, sturdy and durable; it should be unobtrusive in design, so that it helps to give a quiet and harmonious background to the furnishings of the room, and its coloring should be soft and subdued, repeating the tones that prevail throughout the general decorative scheme. We illustrate here a few of the rugs that are made for us after our own designs and in colors chosen by ourselves. The only exception is the Donegal rug, which is made in Ireland after the designs of Voysey and his school

Donegal Rug. Section of design shown in illustration. The colors are usually forest and leather tones of green and brown, with designs based on conventional plant forms. The material used is a high grade wool, and the rugs are hand-tufted and are finished with a thick firm pile. These rugs are made in any size to order

Price, per Square Yard - - - - - - - - - - $13.50

India Drugget Rug. A firm, heavy, hand-woven rug which we carry in colors and patterns made especially for us, and carefully designed with reference to its harmony with Craftsman furnishings. The illustration here shows our Nile design, but we carry the rugs also in a scroll pattern on a plain ground. One has a green scroll with plain green band, another a blue scroll and band, and others have light colored scrolls with green and blue background. The Nile design comes in natural background, with the design carried out in soft tones of brown and blue. These rugs are made in India of bullocks' wool and are reversible

Dimensions and prices of India Drugget Rugs in the scroll pattern in any of the colors described

3	x	3	- - - -	$5.50
5	x	3	- - - -	7.75
6	x	3	- - - -	10.00
9	x	6	- - - -	28.50
12	x	9	- - - -	57.00
15	x	12	- - - -	95.00

Dimensions and prices of India Drugget Rugs in Nile Design

3	x	3	- - - -	$5.50
5	x	3	- - - -	7.75
6	x	3	- - - -	10.00
7	x	5	- - - -	19.00
9	x	6	- - - -	28.50
12	x	9	- - - -	57.00
12	x	12	- - - -	76.00
13	x	10	- - - -	68.00
15	x	12	- - - -	95.00

INDIA DRUGGET RUG IN NILE DESIGN

Regular Craftsman Rug. Woven for us from specially selected Scotch yarn. The design is our own and is worked out in three different color combinations, one rug showing a ground of deep leaf green with the design in wood and leather tones, while another has a ground of dark brown almost the color of old oak, with the design worked out in lighter wood brown and straw color. A third has a ground of dark blue with the design in lighter shades of the same color

Dimensions and prices of the Regular Craftsman Rug

3 x 5	- - - - - -	$5.00
3 x 6	- - - - - -	6.00
6 x 9	- - - - - -	18.00
7½ x 10½	- - - - - -	26.00
9 x 12	- - - - - -	36.00
10½ x 13½	- - - - - -	47.00
12 x 15	- - - - - -	60.00

New Craftsman Rug. This is the latest addition to the Craftsman line and has proven particularly satisfactory. The illustration shows the design, but can give no idea of the coloring which is specially attractive, as the design is worked out in green on a background of deep brown, broken here and there with spots of light golden brown. The rug is made of wool and is very durable and substantial

Dimensions and prices of New Craftsman Rug

3 x 6 - - - - - - -	$5.00
6 x 9 - - - - - - -	15.00
9 x 10½ - - - - - - -	26.50
9 x 12 - - - - - - -	30.00

The reason that we recommended these rugs to be used in connection with the Craftsman scheme of decoration lies in the fact that they have a certain strength and simplicity which brings them into closer harmony with the Craftsman furniture and woodwork than would be the case with the more delicately colored and intricately designed rugs that are so well suited to the lighter and more elaborate styles of furnishing. As all Craftsman furniture is made of oak, and as the interior woodwork of a Craftsman room corresponds in character to the furniture, it follows that so important a part of the furnishing as a rug would naturally show coloring based for the most part upon the wood and leaf tones and a texture that is in keeping with the sturdy fibre and dull mellow surface of the wood

THE WORK OF
L & J. G. STICKLEY
FAYETTEVILLE, NEW YORK

THE numerous pieces that furnish your house — the Chairs, the Tables, the oaken Settles, Sideboards and all the others—are undoubtedly THINGS! Yes, but if you choose each piece with due regard to your individual needs and preferences, if you carefully create an environment of furniture; each piece of it then becomes, not a THING, but an undeniable part of yourself!

Individuality

¶ L. & J. G. Stickley, makers of the simple and entirely American type of furniture that bears their impress, are working for individuals. Each year sees many new designs taking shapes of wood and leather in their shops, built, every one of them, to take an intimate place in some household or to serve someone in a public building; skilfully contrived, that is, to fit an individual need.

Harmony

¶ You demand in your house, in your office or in your public building, a certain well-defined harmony. Wall treatment, floors, furniture, must all harmonize in color and pattern, must bear a subtle relationship to each other. In response to this demand of yours for harmony, the furniture illustrated in this little book is planned and fashioned to fit into your scheme, whatever that may be.

Woods

¶ White oak, the wood chiefly used, is selected not only for strength and durability, but on account of a capacity for taking on various shades and tones of color.

Design

¶ This oak, cut in the forests of Kentucky, is built into furniture strong and durable, though not over heavy, suitable for your office, bank, or for the more formal rooms of your house; or slighter shapes are wrought from the oak, showing in their details graceful curves and variations of surface, perhaps bits of inlay in the same wood; or again the oak is turned into a little masterpiece of downright invention, as for instance the Davenport bed No. 285 on pages 28 and 29, an invention that makes for your comfort.

Finishes

¶ A design fitted for some particular need of yours decided upon (and there are whole groups of furniture with the same motive running through them, suitable for use together in a room) the question of harmonizing color and finish is developed in the L. & J. G. Stickley Shops. And in this field of endeavor Leopold Stickley, "L" of the firm, one of the well known family of master workers in wood, has through several years of study and experiment arrived at expert knowledge of possible colors and undertones, treating the oak through fuming and staining, producing beauty of color as rich and glowing as that found upon certain old canvases.

Texture

¶ Fumed by ammonia in air-tight compartments, and stained in tones that show beautiful undertints, the furniture is next given, through sanding and waxing, a smooth bloom-like texture, so that the arm or back of your chair is delightful to the touch.

Leathers

¶ In treating the leathers used as covering for chair cushions or table tops, colors harmonizing or contrasting with those of the furniture are obtained, giving the needful accents to your color scheme. Old time methods of tanning are used, and no injurious acids impair the strength of the leather. Goat skins, not long since on their former owners, roaming the meadows of Palestine, thus contribute to the beauty and comfort of your rooms, since the skins used in the Work of L. & J. G. Stickley come from those sections of the Holy Land where the finest goats in the world are grown. Native hides are used for large table tops, and fabrics plain and figured are occasionally employed for cushion coverings.

Metal Work

¶ Where hinges and pulls are needed, as upon chests of drawers and bookcases, these metal fixtures are of copper handwrought in simple designs. The copper is hammered to obtain texture and is dulled and modulated in color by various processes until the soft tones of old metal are secured.

Details of Construction

¶ How your furniture is built is a matter of vital importance to you. Furniture of simple and good construction does not go out of style in a few years, but lasts your lifetime. The Work of L. & J. G. Stickley, built in a scientific manner, does not attempt to follow the traditions of a bygone day. All the resources of modern invention are used as helps in constructing this thoroughly modern product, more suitable, as many notable authorities believe, to the house of to-day—your house, that is—than is the furniture of past centuries or its necessarily machine made reproductions.

¶ If you examine the table legs and those of the large chairs built at the L. & J. G. Stickley Shops, you will find that each side of the post is quarter sawed. If you should investigate further and cut a cross section through the post, you will find that it is not veneered but built of four pieces of solid oak, with a tiny core, all so tightly welded together that no cracking is possible, and the post is practically indestructible, while the fine silver flake of the quartering is seen from any point of view. Table tops, necessarily constructed, in these days of narrow boards, of several pieces of lumber, are fastened together by "splines" or tiny wedges as you see in the drawing or in your table top, so that no splitting is possible, the splines giving an agreeable bit of structural ornament.

¶ Cushions are built on steel and securely fastened to wooden frames. This construction, used in the making of automobile seats, is original in its use for furniture with the Work of L. & J. G. Stickley and has

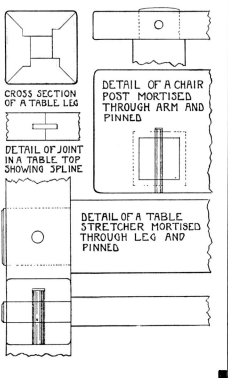

CROSS SECTION OF A TABLE LEG

DETAIL OF JOINT IN A TABLE TOP SHOWING SPLINE

DETAIL OF A CHAIR POST MORTISED THROUGH ARM AND PINNED

DETAIL OF A TABLE STRETCHER MORTISED THROUGH LEG AND PINNED

in the years since its adoption proved eminently satisfactory. The seat cushions are removable, slipping easily into place; they are exceedingly comfortable, the cushions keep their shape and the leather lasts much longer than in a springless cushion. Back cushions are ventilated through air holes. When pressure is applied to the cushions the air is expelled. When relieved of pressure the cushion becomes filled with air, which penetrates the filling, keeping it well ventilated. Back cushions are kept in place by leather straps, so that they do not annoy you by falling out of place.

Comfort

¶ In these details and in many others care is given to your comfort, as well as to the durability of each piece of furniture. Chairs are studied from the point of view of many different sitters, and are of many sizes and proportions. In planning the height of tables, and especially of desks, an average is not struck. Heights suitable to various individuals are carefully planned.

The Makers Have no Other Occupation

¶ The Work of L. & J. G. Stickley is a product that claims and fills the entire time of its producers, who indulge in no other occupation, rightly thinking that each process, from the proper seasoning of the timber to the exact color to be attained in the finished piece, must be watched to guard against the slightest measure of failure and to secure the greatest possible efficiency of method. Furniture building, it is believed, is in itself an important work, demanding the entire time of the modern craftsmen who attempt it.

¶ At the New York office at 815 Marbridge Building, Herald Square, J. George Stickley, the other member of the firm, has in charge that important branch of the Work, the placing of the finished pieces of furniture in various shops and stores where you may see and buy them. Each piece you may find, in New York or Boston, in Honolulu, South Africa, or any other of the various cities or countries that demand it, has imprinted upon it the device

The Work *of* L. & J. G. Stickley

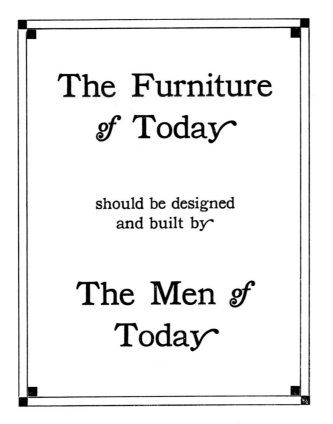

The Furniture
of Today

should be designed
and built by

The Men *of*
Today

⊞ THE WORK OF L&J.G. STICKLEY

950 Chair

Height, 35 in.   Width, 16¾ in.   Wood seat

1350, the same with leather upholstered or flag seat

Rockers to match 1351 and 951

950

1351

504

504 Table	-	-	-	28 x 42 in.
505 Table, same design as 504				30 x 48 in.
506 Table, same design as 504				32 x 54 in.
510 Table, same design as 504				36 x 60 in.
511 Table,	-	-	-	36 x 72 in.

1352

1352 Arm Chair

Height, 37½ in. Width, 20¾ in. Leather upholstered or flag seat

952, the same with wood seat

Rockers to match 953 and 1353

558

953

203 Settle

Height, 37½ in. Width, 39½ in. Wood seat

205, the same with leather upholstered seat

558 Tabourette

Height, 17 in. Top, 15 x 15 in.

203

511

6

1340 Chair
Height, 35¾ in.
Width, 17¾ in.
Leather upholstered or flag seat
940, the same with wood seat
Rockers to match 1341 and 941

1340

942 Arm Chair
Height, 37½ in.
Width, 21¼ in.
Wood seat

942

581

581 Table
Height, 29 in.   Diameter, 42 in.

559

559 Tabourette
Height, 20 in.   Top, 18 x 18 in.

941

1342, same as 942 with leather upholstered or flag seat
Rockers to match 1343 and 943

1343

598

598 Table
Height, 29 in.   Top, 30 x 48 in.
Blind drawer

597 Table
Same design as 598
Top, 28 x 40 in.

206 Settle
Height, 37½ in.
Width, 39½ in.
Leather upholstered seat
204, the same with wood seat

206

7

800 Chair
Height, 36¼ in.　Width, 18¼ in.
Spring cushion seat

801 Rocker
To match 800 Chair

800

802

801

802 Arm Chair
Height, 37½ in.　Width, 21¾ in.
Spring cushion seat

803 Arm Rocker
To match 802 Arm Chair

808 Chair
Height, 38½ in.　Width, 18¼ in.
Spring cushion seat

809 Rocker
To match 808 Chair

808

803

809

810 Arm Chair
Height, 39 in.　Width, 21¾ in.
Spring cushion seat

811 Arm Rocker
To match 810 Arm Chair

810

811

FAYETTEVILLE, NEW YORK

848

846

849

848 Arm Chair
Height, 37½ in.
Width, 21½ in.
Spring cushion seat

849 Arm Rocker
To match 848 Arm Chair

846 Chair
Height, 36½ in.   Width, 18½ in.
Spring cushion seat

847 Rocker
To match 846 Chair

818 Arm Chair
Height, 39 in.   Width, 22¾ in.
Spring cushion seat

819 Arm Rocker
To match 818 Arm Chair

818

819

847

817

816 Arm Chair
Height, 39 in.   Width, 22¾ in.
Spring cushion seat

817 Arm Rocker
To match 816 Arm Chair

816

9

THE WORK OF L&J.G.STICKLEY

573 Table - - - 18 in. diameter
575 Table, same design as 573, 24 in. diameter
577 Table, same design as 573, 30 in. diameter
579 Table - - - 36 in. diameter

820

820 Chair
Height, 36 in. Width, 19¾ in.
Spring cushion seat

579

821

821 Rocker
To match 820 Chair

225 Settle
Height, 36½ in. Width, 48 in.
Depth, 20½ in.
Spring cushion seat

560 Tabourette
Height, 18 in.
Top, 16 x 16 in.

225

573

560

822 Arm Chair
Height, 36½ in. Width, 23 in.
Spring cushion seat

823 Arm Rocker
To match 822 Arm Chair

822

823

10

FAYETTEVILLE, NEW YORK

824

580

825

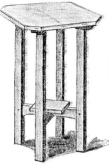

574

824 Chair
Height, 36 in.   Width, 19½ in.
Spring cushion seat

825 Rocker, to match 824 chair
574 Table - - - - - 18 x 18 in.
576 Table, same design as 574, 24 x 24 in.
578 Table, same design as 574, 30 x 30 in.
580 Table - - - - - 36 x 36 in.

226 Settle
Height, 36½ in.   Width, 48 in.
Depth, 20½ in.   Spring cushion seat

561 Tabourette
Height, 20 in.   Top, 18 x 18 in.

226

826

561

826 Arm Chair
Height, 36½ in.
Width, 23 in.
Spring cushion
seat

827 Arm Rocker
To match 826
Arm Chair

827

11

◧ THE WORK OF L&J.G.STICKLEY

842 Chair
Height, 36 in.   Width, 19¾ in.
Spring cushion seat

843 Rocker
To match 842 Chair

842

465

843

465 Arm Rocker
Height, 37 in.
Width, 22¾ in.
Spring cushion seat

227 Settle
Height, 36½ in.
Width, 48 in.
Depth, 20½ in.
Spring cushion seat

562 Tabourette
Height, 22 in.
Top, 20 x 20 in.

227

562

844

587

845

587 Drink Stand
Height, 27 in.
Top, 16 x 16 in.

844 Arm Chair
Height, 36½ in.   Width, 23 in.
Spring cushion seat

845 Arm Rocker
To match 844 Arm Chair

FAYETTEVILLE, NEW YORK

24 Plant Stand

Height, 28 in.
Width, 13½ in.
Depth, 13½ in.

508 Tea Table

Height, 24 in.
Diameter, 24 in.

25 Plant Stand

Height, 22 in.
Width, 13½ in.
Depth, 13½ in.

507 Tea Table

Height, 24 in.
Top, 17 x 26 in.

24

508

25

509 Drop Leaf Tea Table

Height, 24 in.
Top, 24 x 24 in.
With leaves down,
6 x 24 in.

836 Arm Chair

Height, 44 in.
Width, 22¾ in.
Spring cushion seat.

837 Arm Rocker

To match 836 Arm
Chair

509

507

52

52 Chafing Dish Stand

Height, 28 in.   Top, 12 x 18 in.

837

836

13

424 Chair
Height, 36 in.
Width, 19½ in.
Spring cushion seat

425 Rocker
To match 424 Chair

424

425

545

536 Table	- - -	diameter, 24 in.
537 Table, same design as 536,		diameter, 36 in.
538 Table, same design as 536,		diameter, 30 in.
539 Table, same design as 536,		diameter, 42 in.
544 Table, same design as 536,		diameter, 48 in.
545 Table	- - -	diameter, 54 in.

422 Arm Chair
Height, 38 in.   Width, 24 in.
Spring cushion seat

423 Arm Rocker
To match 422 Arm Chair

422

423

262 Settle
Height, 38½ in.
Width, 72 in.
Depth, 24 in.
Spring cushion
seat

261 Settle
Same design
as 262
Height, 38½ in.
Width, 60 in.
Depth, 24 in.

260 Settle
Same design
as 262
Height, 38½ in.
Width, 48 in.
Depth, 23 in.

536

262

14

FAYETTEVILLE, NEW YORK

436 Arm Chair
Height, 40 in.
Width, 24 in.
Spring cushion seat
437 Arm Rocker
To match 436 Arm
  Chair

489
Arm Rocker
Height, 41 in.
Width, 24 in.
Spring cushion
  seat

840 Arm Chair
Height, 39 in.
Width, 22⅞ in.
Spring cushion seat
841 Arm Rocker
To match 840 Arm
  Chair

27 Pedestal
Height, 36 in.
Top, 12 x 12 in.
28 Pedestal
Same design as 27
Height, 42 in.
Top, 13 x 13 in.

437

541

489

840

841

27 and 28

540 Table, same design as 541,
  diameter, 24 in.
541 Table - - diameter, 30 in.
542 Table, same design as 541,
  diameter, 36 in.
543 Table - - diameter, 42 in.

436

543

THE WORK OF L&J.G.STICKLEY

488 Arm Chair
Height, 47 in.
Width, 24 in.
Spring cushion seat

487 Arm Rocker
To match 488 Arm
Chair

407 Arm Rocker
Height, 40 in.
Width, 22¾ in.
Spring cushion seat

488

487

407

450

451

450 Arm Chair
Height, 40 in.
Width, 24 in.
Spring cushion seat

451 Arm Rocker
To match 450 Arm
Chair

404 Arm Chair
Height, 37 in.
Width, 22¾ in.
Spring cushion seat

405 Arm Rocker
To match 404 Arm
Chair

404

405

FAYETTEVILLE, NEW YORK ▣

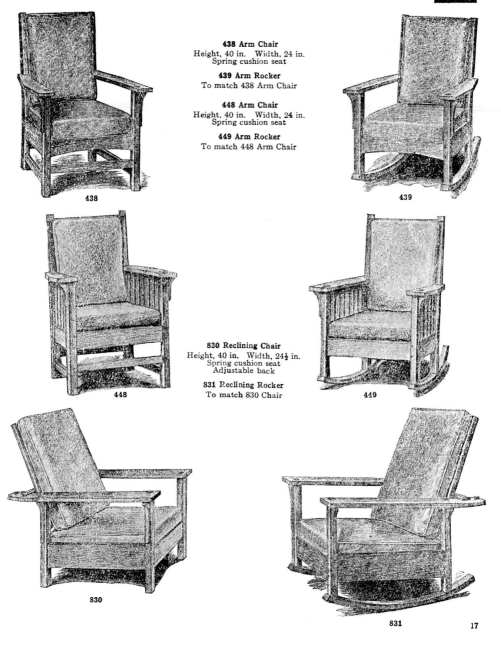

438 Arm Chair
Height, 40 in. Width, 24 in.
Spring cushion seat

439 Arm Rocker
To match 438 Arm Chair

448 Arm Chair
Height, 40 in. Width, 24 in.
Spring cushion seat

449 Arm Rocker
To match 448 Arm Chair

830 Reclining Chair
Height, 40 in. Width, 24½ in.
Spring cushion seat
Adjustable back

831 Reclining Rocker
To match 830 Chair

438

439

448

449

830

831

17

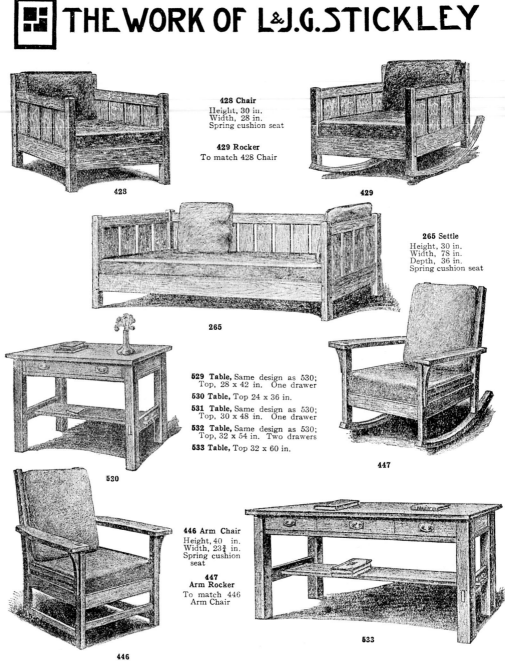

⊞ THE WORK OF L&J.G.STICKLEY

428 Chair
Height, 30 in.
Width, 28 in.
Spring cushion seat

429 Rocker
To match 428 Chair

428

429

265 Settle
Height, 30 in.
Width, 78 in.
Depth, 36 in.
Spring cushion seat

265

529 Table, Same design as 530;
Top, 28 x 42 in.   One drawer

530 Table, Top 24 x 36 in.

531 Table, Same design as 530;
Top, 30 x 48 in.   One drawer

532 Table, Same design as 530;
Top, 32 x 54 in.   Two drawers

533 Table, Top 32 x 60 in.

447

530

446 Arm Chair
Height, 40   in.
Width, 23¾ in.
Spring cushion
seat

**447
Arm Rocker**
To match 446
Arm Chair

446

533

18

FAYETTEVILLE, NEW YORK

452

453

452 Arm Chair

Height, 40 in.
Width, 23¾ in.
Spring cushion seat

453 Arm Rocker

To match 452 Arm
Chair

524

520

520 Table
Top, 24 x 36 in.
521 Table
Same design as 520
Top, 28 x 42 in., one drawer
522 Table
Same design as 520
Top, 30 x 48 in., two drawers
523 Table
Same design as 520
Top, 32 x 54 in., two drawers
524 Table
Top, 32 x 60 in.

471

475

471 Reclining Chair

Height, 40 in.
Width, 25¾ in.
Spring cushion seat
Adjustable back

475 Reclining Rocker

To match 471 Chair
Stationary back

420 Arm Chair
Height, 42 in.
Width, 25½ in.
Spring cushion seat

421 Arm Rocker
To match 420 Arm
   Chair

420

421

411 Reclining Chair
Height, 40 in.
Width, 27½ in.
Spring cushion seat
Stationary back

412 Reclining Chair
Height, 40 in.
Width, 27 in.
Spring cushion seat
Adjustable back

412

413 Reclining Rocker
To match 411 Chair
Stationary back

470 Reclining Chair
Same as 411
Adjustable back

411

413

FAYETTEVILLE, NEW YORK

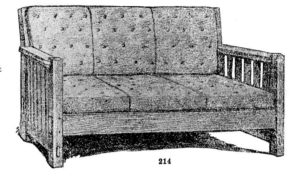

408 Arm Chair
Height, 32 in.
Width, 25 in.
Spring cushion seat

409 Arm Rocker
To match 408 Arm
Chair

214 Settle
Height, 32½ in.
Width, 60 in.
Spring cushion seat

214

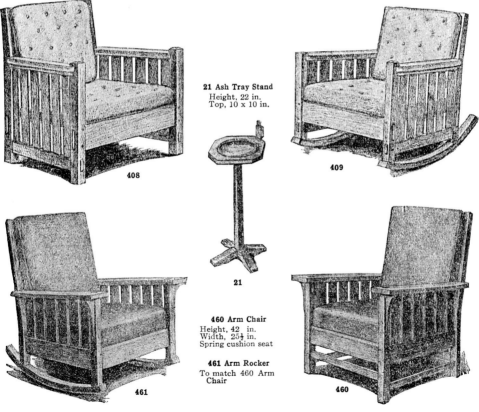

21 Ash Tray Stand
Height, 22 in.
Top, 10 x 10 in.

408

409

21

460 Arm Chair
Height, 42 in.
Width, 25½ in.
Spring cushion seat

461 Arm Rocker
To match 460 Arm
Chair

461

460

21

394 Stool
Height, 16 in. Width, 19¼ in.
Leather upholstered

410 Reclining Chair
Height, 40 in. Width, 27 in.
Spring cushion seat
Adjustable back

426 Arm Chair
Height, 42 in. Width, 25½ in.
Spring cushion seat

427 Arm Rocker
To match 426 Arm Chair

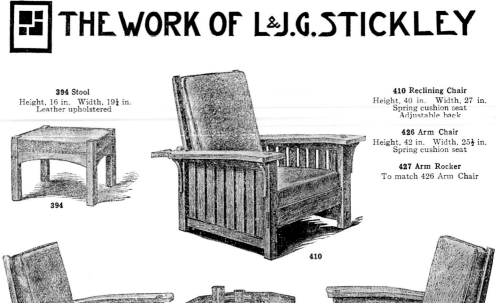

394

410

427

515

426

**498 Reclining
Chair**
Height, 40 in.
Width, 27½ in.
Spring cushion
seat
Adjustable back

**497 Reclining
Chair**
Same as 498
Stationary back

395

395 Stool
Height, 9 in.
Width, 19 in.
Leather uphol-
stered

515 Smokers' Stand
Height, 24 in.
Top, 20 x 20 in.

498

497

22

FAYETTEVILLE, NEW YORK

389

389 Stool
Height, 15½ in.   Width, 21 in.
Spring cushion seat

396 Stool
Height, 16 in.   Width, 20 in.
Leather upholstered

397 Stool
Height, 16 in.   Width, 20 in.
Spring cushion seat

480

481

480 Arm Chair
Height, 38 in.   Width, 25 in.
Spring cushion seat and back

481 Arm Rocker
To match 480 Arm Chair

396

485 Arm Rocker
Height, 41½ in.   Width, 25½ in.
Spring cushion seat

400 Arm Chair
Height, 41 in.   Width, 27 in.
Spring cushion seat

401 Arm Rocker
To match 400 Arm Chair

397

485

400

401

23

THE WORK OF L&J.G.STICKLEY

482 Arm Chair
Height, 39½ in.
Width, 27½ in.
Spring cushion
    seat and back

483 Arm Rocker
To match 482
    Arm Chair

266 Settle
Height, 39½ in.
Width, 72 in.
Depth, 29 in.
Spring cushion
    seat and back

482

383

483

563

266

383 Stool
Height, 4 in. Top, 8½ x 14 in.
    Leather upholstered

563 Table
Height, 29 in. Top, 48 x 48 in.

416

416 Arm Chair

Height, 27 in.
Width, 39 in. over
    all
Depth, 35 in. over
    all
Spring cushion seat

220 Settle

Height, 29 in.
Width, 84½ in. over
    all
Depth, 36¾ in. over
    all
Spring cushion seat

220

24

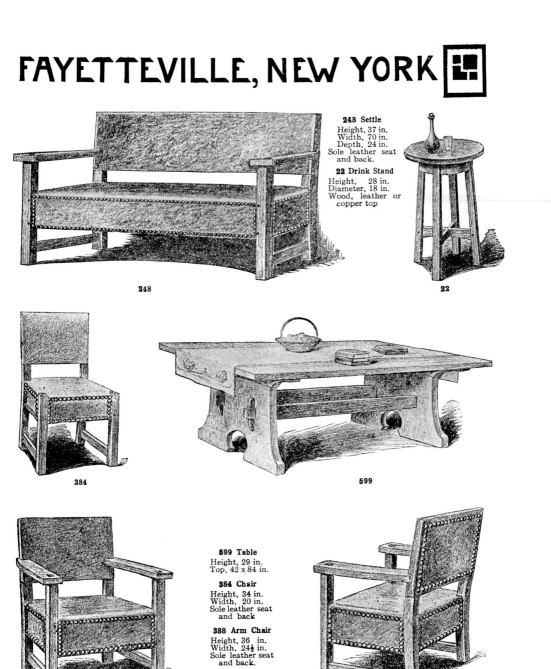

248 Settle
Height, 37 in.
Width, 70 in.
Depth, 24 in.
Sole leather seat
and back.

22 Drink Stand
Height, 28 in.
Diameter, 18 in.
Wood, leather or
copper top

248

22

384

599

599 Table
Height, 29 in.
Top, 42 x 84 in.

384 Chair
Height, 34 in.
Width, 20 in.
Sole leather seat
and back

388 Arm Chair
Height, 36 in.
Width, 24½ in.
Sole leather seat
and back.

388

388 (back view)

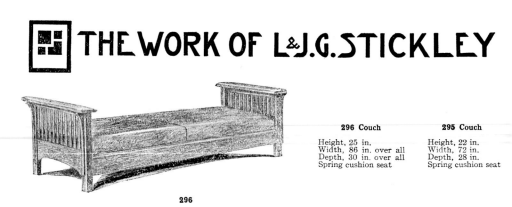

296

296 Couch

Height, 25 in.
Width, 86 in. over all
Depth, 30 in. over all
Spring cushion seat

295 Couch

Height, 22 in.
Width, 72 in.
Depth, 28 in.
Spring cushion seat

554 Tabourette

Height, 16 in.
Top, 12 x 12 in.

555 Tabourette

Same design as 554
Height, 18 in.
Top, 15 x 15 in.

556 Tabourette

Same design as 554
Height, 20 in.
Top, 18 x 18 in.

554

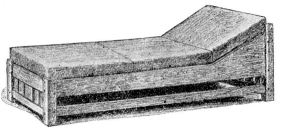

295

292

557 Tabourette

Height, 22 in.
Top, 21 x 21 in.

557

292 Couch

Height, 28 in.
Width, 80 in.
Depth, 30 in.
Spring cushion seat

291 Couch

Height, 26 in.
Width, 76 in.
Depth, 30 in.
Spring cushion seat

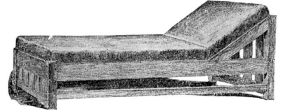

291

FAYETTEVILLE, NEW YORK

232 Settle

Height, 28 in.
Width, 72 in.
Depth, 27 in.
Spring cushion seat

232

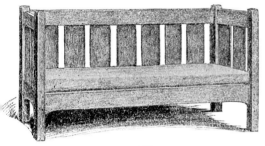

216

216 Settle

Height, 36 in.
Width, 72 in.
Depth, 26 in.
Spring cushion seat

218 Swing

Same as 216 Settle
Height, 30 in.

215 Settle

Same design as 216
Height, 36 in.
Width, 54 in.
Depth, 24 in.
Spring cushion seat

217 Swing

Same as 215 Settle
Height, 30 in.

234 Settle

Height, 25½ in.
Width, 86 in. over all
Depth, 34 in. over all
Spring cushion seat

234

263

263 Settle

Height, 37 in.
Width, 72 in.
Depth, 25 in.
Spring cushion seat

THE WORK OF L&J.G.STICKLEY

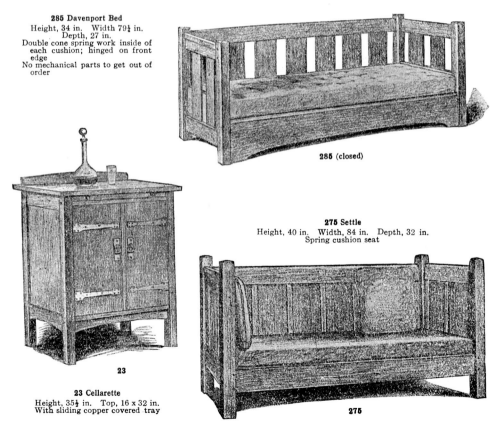

281 Settle
Height, 34 in. Width, 76 in. Depth, 31 in.
Spring cushion seat

280 Settle
Same design as 281
Height, 34 in. Width, 60 in. Depth, 31 in.
Spring cushion seat

285 Davenport Bed
Height, 34 in. Width 79¼ in.
Depth, 27 in.
Double cone spring work inside of each cushion; hinged on front edge
No mechanical parts to get out of order

285 (closed)

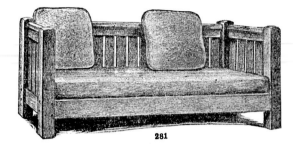

275 Settle
Height, 40 in. Width, 84 in. Depth, 32 in.
Spring cushion seat

23

23 Cellarette
Height, 35½ in. Top, 16 x 32 in.
With sliding copper covered tray

275

28

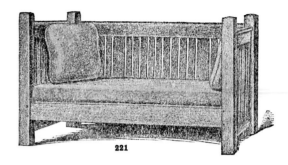

221 Settle
Height, 39 in.   Width, 60 in.   Depth, 30 in.
Spring cushion seat

221

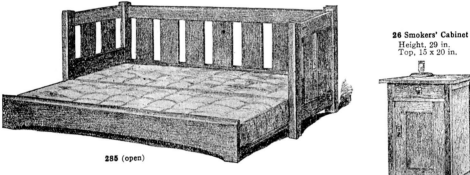

285 (open)

26 Smokers' Cabinet
Height, 29 in.
Top, 15 x 20 in.

26

222 Settle
Height, 39 in.   Width, 76 in.   Depth, 31 in.
Spring cushion seat

223 Settle
Same design as 222
Height, 39 in.   Width, 84 in.   Depth, 32 in.
Spring cushion seat

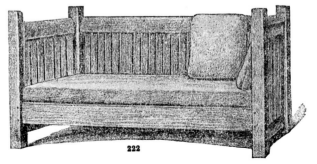

222

THE WORK OF L&J.G.STICKLEY

100

100 Mirror
Glass, 20 x 40 in.

589

589 Tip Table
Height,   24 in.
Diameter. 20 in.

582

582 Table
Height, 29 in.
Top, 42 x 42 in.

551

551 Sewing Table
Height, 29 in.
Top closed, 16 x 20 in.
Top open, 16 x 44 in.
Top drawer fitted with
cedar tray

553 Drop Leaf Table
Height, 30 in.
Diameter of top open, 42 in.
With leaves down, 14 x 42 in.

552 Drop Leaf Table
Height, 30 in.
Top open, 42 x 42 in.
With leaves down, 14 x 42 in.

553

552

588 Tip Table
Height, 28¼ in.
Top, 28 x 28 in.

588

517 Table
Height, 29 in.
Top, 19 x 40 in.

1341 Rocker
Height, 33½ in.
Width, 17¾ in.
Leather upholstered
or flag seat

1341

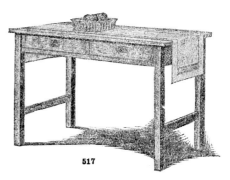

517

519 Folding Table
Height, 30 in.
Top, 18 x 36 in.
Top open, 36 x 36 in.

519 (open)

519 (closed)

599

599 Table
Height, 29 in.
Top, 32 x 48 in.

599

599 Table
Height, 29 in.
Top, 32 x 60 in.
Also made 32 x 54 in.

593

593 Table
Height, 29 in.
Top, 30 x 48 in.

595 and 596

596 Table
Height, 29 in.
Top, 36 x 60 in.

595 Table
Same design as 596
Top, 36 x 54 in.

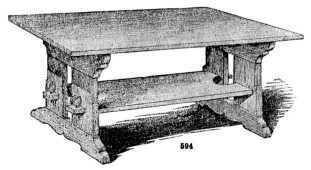

594

594 Table
Height, 29 in.
Top, 45 x 72 in.

601 Desk
Height, 34½ in.
Top, 20 x 34 in.

602 Desk
Height, 36½ in.
Top, 22 x 40 in.

604 Desk
Height, 36¼ in.
Top, 22 x 40 in.

601

602

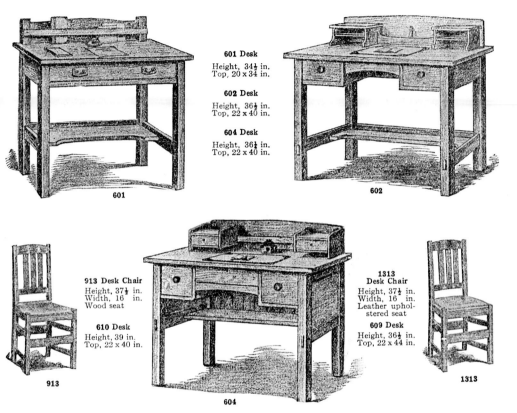

913 Desk Chair
Height, 37½ in.
Width, 16 in.
Wood seat

610 Desk
Height, 39 in.
Top, 22 x 40 in.

**1313
Desk Chair**
Height, 37½ in.
Width, 16 in.
Leather uphol-
stered seat

609 Desk
Height, 36½ in.
Top, 22 x 44 in.

913

1313

604

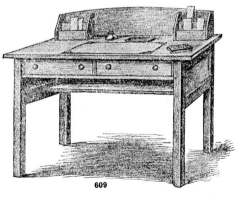

610

609

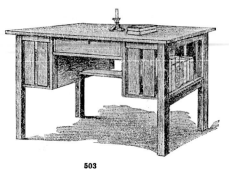

503

503 Desk

Height, 30 in. Top, 28 x 42 in.

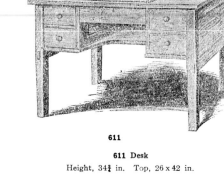

611

611 Desk

Height, 34¼ in. Top, 26 x 42 in.

502

502 Desk

Height, 30 in. Top, 28 x 48 in.

501

501 Desk

Height, 30 in. Top, 30 x 48 in.

500 Desk

Same design as 501. Top, 26 x 42 in.

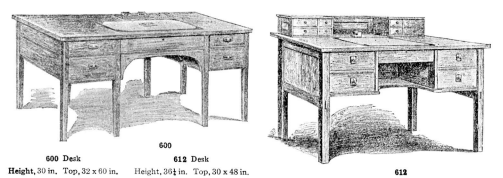

600

600 Desk

Height, 30 in. Top, 32 x 60 in.

612 Desk

Height, 36½ in. Top, 30 x 48 in.

612

34

FAYETTEVILLE, NEW YORK ⌊F⌉

386 Office Chair
Height, 36 in.
Width, 19 in.
Sole leather seat

616
Typewriter Desk
Made in two sizes
Height, 30 in.
Top, 32 x 39 in.
Top, 32 x 44 in.

386

616

615

387 Office Chair
Height, 38 in.
Width, 21 in.
Sole leather seat

615 Desk
Height, 30 in.
Top, 34 x 60 in.

614 Roll Top Desk
Height, 43 in.
Top, 34 x 60 in.

387

850 Office Chair
Height, 38 in.
Width, 23 in.
Spring cushion
seat

20 Waste Basket
Height, 16 in.
Size at top, 13 x 13 in.

850

20

614

THE WORK OF L&J.G.STICKLEY

613 Desk
Height, 40½ in.   Width, 32 in.
Writing bed, 16½ x 30 in.

660 Desk
Height, 39¾ in.   Width, 29¾ in.
Writing bed, 19½ x 25¾ in.

40 Magazine Stand
Height, 44 in.   Top, 13 x 23½ in.

41 Magazine Stand
Height, 30 in.   Top, 12 x 36 in.

46 Magazine Stand
Height, 42 in.   Width, 21 in.

613

660

41

40

46

661 Desk

Height, 44½ in.
Width, 42 in.
Writing bed, 27 x 37 in.

639 Book Case
Height, 48 in.
Top, 13½ x 60 in.

639

661

36

FAYETTEVILLE, NEW YORK

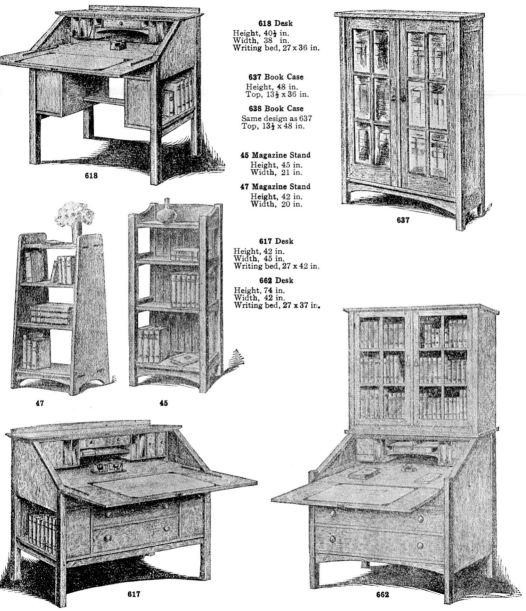

618 Desk
Height, 40½ in.
Width, 38 in.
Writing bed, 27 x 36 in.

637 Book Case
Height, 48 in.
Top, 13½ x 36 in.

638 Book Case
Same design as 637
Top, 13½ x 48 in.

45 Magazine Stand
Height, 45 in.
Width, 21 in.

47 Magazine Stand
Height, 42 in.
Width, 20 in.

617 Desk
Height, 42 in.
Width, 45 in.
Writing bed, 27 x 42 in.

662 Desk
Height, 74 in.
Width, 42 in.
Writing bed, 27 x 37 in.

618

637

47

45

617

662

37

THE WORK OF L&J.G.STICKLEY

645

516 Book Table

Height, 29 in.
Top, 27 x 27 in.

641

645 Book Case
Height, 55 in.   Width, 49 in.
646 Book Shelves
Same as 645 without doors
647 Book Case
Height, 55 in.   Width, 70 in.
648 Book Shelves
Same as 647 without doors

516

641 Book Case
Height, 55 in.   Width, 30 in.
642 Book Shelves
Same as 641 without door
643 Book Case
Same design as 641
Height, 55 in.   Width, 36 in.
Two doors
644 Book Shelves
Same as 643 without doors

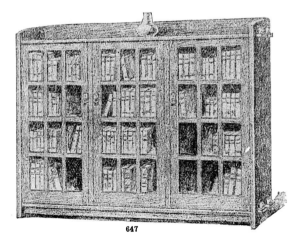

647

653 Book Case
Height, 55 in.
Width at top,
27 in.

653

38

652

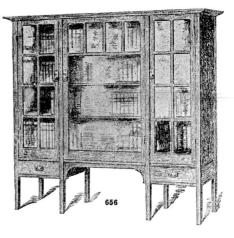

656

652 Book Case
Height, 51¼ in.
Width, 22 in

654 Book Case
Height, 55 in.
Width at top, 50 in.

656 Book Case
Height, 66 in.   Top, 14½ x 72 in.

657 Book Case
Height, 66 in.   Top, 14½ x 26 in.

655 Book Case
Height, 55 in.   Width at top, 74 in.

657

654

655

THE WORK OF L&J.G.STICKLEY

958 Dining Arm Chair
Height, 36½ in.
Width, 19¾ in.
Wood seat

956 Dining Chair
Height, 35 in.
Width, 16¾ in.
Wood seat

707 Sideboard
Height, 43¾ in.
Top, 20 x 48 in.

760 China Closet
Height, 60 in.
Top, 16 x 36 in.

958

956

751

751 Serving Table
Height, 33½ in.   Top, 16 x 32 in.
Blind drawer

707

722 Dining Table
Diameter, 48 in.
To extend 6 and
8 feet

1356 Dining Chair
Height, 35 in.
Width, 16¾ in.
Leather uphol-
stered or flag
seat

**1358
Dining Arm Chair**
Height, 36½ in.
Width, 19¾ in.
Leather uphol-
stered or flag
seat

1358, with flag
seat, has long
arms

760

1358

722

1356

40

FAYETTEVILLE, NEW YORK

1352½
Dining Arm Chair
Height, 37½ in.
Width, 20¾ in.
Leather upholstered
seat

952½, the same with
wood seat

1350 Dining Chair
Height, 35 in.
Width, 16¾ in.
Leather upholstered seat

950, the same with
wood seat

734 Sideboard
Height, 44 in.
Top, 20 x 48 in.

727 China Closet
Height, 55 in.
Width, 34 in.
Depth, 15 in.

718 Dining Table
Diameter, 48, 54
and 60 in.
To extend 8, 10
and 12 ft.

1352

1350

734

727

1352 Flag Seat

718

1350 Flag Seat

942½ Dining Arm Chair
Height, 37½ in.
Width, 21¾ in.
Wood seat

940 Dining Chair
Height, 35¾ in.
Width, 17¾ in.
Wood seat

752 Serving Table
Height, 38½ in.
Top, 15 x 40 in.

720 Dining Table
Diameter, 48, 54 and 60 in.
To extend 8, 10 and 12 ft.

752

942½

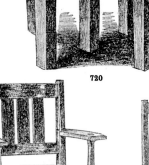

1342½ Dining Arm Chair
Height, 37½ in.
Width, 21¾ in.
Leather upholstered seat

1340 Dining Chair
Height, 35¾ in.
Width, 17¾ in.
Leather upholstered seat

728 China Closet
Height, 55 in.
Width, 48 in.
Depth, 15 in.

720

940

1342½

1340

728

FAYETTEVILLE, NEW YORK

746

800

802

746 China Closet
Height, 62 in.
Top, 16 x 44 in.

716 Dining Table
Diameter, 45 and 48 in.
45 in. to extend 6 ft.
48 in. to extend 6 and 8 ft.

716

800 Dining Chair
Height, 36½ in.
Width, 18¼ in.
Spring cushion seat

802 Dining Arm Chair
Height, 37½ in.
Width, 21¾ in.
Spring cushion seat

808

808 Dining Chair
Height, 38½ in.
Width, 18½ in.
Spring cushion seat

810 Dining Arm Chair
Height, 39 in.
Width, 21¾ in.
Spring cushion seat

709 Sideboard
Height, 48 in.
Top, 22 x 54 in.

810

709

THE WORK OF L&J.G. STICKLEY

362 Dining Arm Chair
Height, 38½ in.   Width, 21¾ in.
Sole leather seat

360 Dining Chair
Height, 36½ in.   Width, 18¼ in.
Sole leather seat

346 Dining Chair
Height, 36½ in.   Width, 18¼ in.
Sole leather seat

348 Dining Arm Chair
Height, 38½ in.   Width, 21¾ in.
Sole leather seat

713 Dining Table
Diameter, 48 and 54 in.   To extend 8, 10 and 12 ft.

362

360

346

713

348

729 China Closet
Height, 70 in.
Top, 17 x 50 in.

736 Sideboard
Height, 48 in.
Top, 22 x 66 in.

735 Sideboard
Same design as 736.
Height, 46 in.
Top, 22 x 56 in.

736

729

44

FAYETTEVILLE, NEW YORK

711

711 Sideboard
Height, 46 in.   Top, 22 x 60 in.

745 Sideboard
Height, 48 in.   Top, 24 x 54 in.

737 Sideboard
Height, 62 in.   Top, 24 x 54 in.
Glass, 14 x 40 in.

745

701

846

701 Dinner Gong
Height, 34¾ in.
Width, 21 in.

846 Dining Chair
Height, 36½ in.
Width, 18¼ in.
Spring cushion
    seat

848 Dining Arm Chair
Height, 37½ in.
Width, 21½ in.
Spring cushion
    seat

848

737

45

741 Serving Table
Height, 39½ in.
Top, 18 x 44 in.

324 Dining Arm Chair
Height, 39 in.
Width, 21 in.
Leather upholstered
slip seat

323 Dining Chair
Height, 38 in.
Width, 18½ in.
Leather upholstered
slip seat

741

324

**820
Dining Chair**
Height, 36 in.
Width, 19¾ in.
Spring cushion
seat

**822 Dining
Arm Chair**
Height, 36½ in.
Width, 23 in.
Spring cushion
seat

731 Sideboard
Height, 49¼ in.
Top, 25 x 72 in.

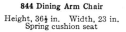

323

820

822

844 Dining Arm Chair
Height, 36½ in.   Width, 23 in.
Spring cushion seat

731

844

740 Serving Table
Height, 49 in.
Top, 22 x 48 in.

824 Dining Chair
Height, 36 in.   Width, 19¾ in.
Spring cushion seat.

740

824

717 Dining Table
Diameter, 48, 54 and
60 in.
To extend 8, 10 and
12 ft.

732 Sideboard
Height, 61½ in.
Top, 25 x 72 in.
Glass, 12 x 58 in.

717

826

826 Dining Arm Chair
Height, 36½ in.
Width, 23 in.
Spring cushion seat

842 Dining Chair
Height, 36 in.
Width, 19¾ in.
Spring cushion seat

842

732

47

950 Chair
Height, 35 in.
Width, 16¾ in.
Wood seat

951 Rocker
To match 950 Chair

951

110 Stand
Height, 29 in.
Top, 14 x 18 in.

110

77

77 Dresser
Height, 69¼ in.
Top, 18½ x 38 in.
Glass, 16 x 24 in.

114

114 Bed
Height of head, 44 in.
Height of foot, 38 in.
Made in standard sizes
Iron side rails

950

115 Bed
Height of head posts, 54 in.
◆Height of foot posts, 48 in.
Made in standard sizes
Iron side rails

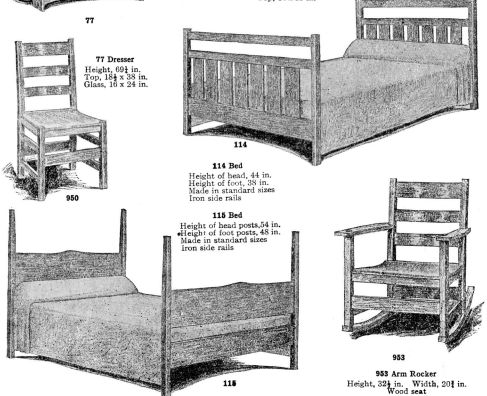

953

953 Arm Rocker
Height, 32½ in.   Width, 20¾ in.
Wood seat

115

FAYETTEVILLE, NEW YORK

1340 Chair
Height, 35¾ in.
Width, 17¾ in.
Leather upholstered seat

1341 Rocker
To match 1340 Chair

1340

1341

1343 Arm Rocker
Height, 35½ in.
Width, 21¾ in.
Leather uphol-
stered seat

1343

550 Table
Height, 29 in.
Top, 18 x 20 in.

97 Chest of Drawers
Height, 40 in.
Top, 18½ x 38 in.

98 Mirror
Glass, 20 x 32 in.

81

81 Dresser
Height, 67 in.
Top, 21 x 44 in.
Glass, 24 x 30 in.

98

550

84 Bed
Height, head post, 54 in.
Height, foot post, 48 in.
Made in standard sizes
Iron side rails

84

97

49

THE WORK OF L&J.G.STICKLEY

90 Chiffonier
Height, 50 in.
Top, 18½ x 42 in.

99 Chest of Drawers
Height, 38 in.
Top, 22 x 48 in.

99

90

93 Dresser
Height, 69 in.
Top, 22 x 48 in.
Glass, 28 x 34 in.

87 Dressing Table
Height, 54¼ in.
Top, 21¼ x 44 in.
Glass, 20 x 34 in.

92 Bed
Height of head posts, 50 in.
Height of foot posts, 44 in.
Made in standard sizes
Iron side rails

87

92

93

FAYETTEVILLE, NEW YORK

102 Chiffonier
Height, 50 in.   Top, 18 x 36 in.

105 Stand
Height, 29½ in.   Top, 14 x 20 in.

101 Dresser
Height, 68 in.   Top, 22 x 54 in.
Glass, 28 x 45 in.

105

102

104 Bed
Height of head, 46 in.
Height of foot, 38 in.
Made in standard sizes
Iron side rails

101

104

103 Dressing Table
Height, 59 in.
Top, 22 x 48 in.
Center glass,
  19½ x 24 in.
Side glasses,
  9 x 20 in.

106 Chest of Drawers
Height, 36 in.
Top, 22 x 54 in.

106

103

95

111 Chiffonier
Height, 48 in.
Top, 19 x 40 in.

95 Umbrella Stand
Height, 29 in.
Width, 21¼ in.
Depth, 12 in.

111

112 Wardrobe
Height, 60 in.
Top, 22½ x 50 in.

112 (open)

112 (closed)

89

89 Costumer
Height, 72 in.

60 Hall Glass
Glass, 18 x 33 in.
Size of frame, 25¾ x 46¼ in.

60

207 Hall Seat
Height, 32 in.
Width, 42 in.
Depth, 18 in.
Drawer under seat

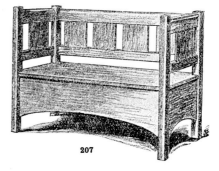

207

61

61 Hall Glass
Center glass, 18 x 28 in.
Side glasses, 10 x 18 in.
Size of frame, 24½ x 55½ in.

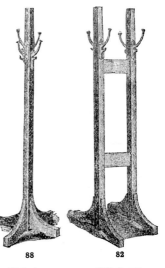

208 Hall Seat
Height, 34 in.
Width, 54 in.
Depth, 18 in.
Drawer under seat

208

88

82

88 Costumer
Height, 72 in.

82 Costumer
Height, 72 in.

53

583 Lunch Table

Height, 30 in.
Diameter, 30 in.

851

583

944

851 Billiard Chair

Height, 42 in.
Width, 23 in.
Spring cushion
seat

950 Chair

Height, 35 in.
Width, 16¾ in.
Wood seat

572 Checker Table

Height, 29 in.
Top, 30 x 30 in.
Checkers, ma-
hogany and
maple

944 Billiard Chair

Height, 43½ in.
Width, 21¾ in.
Wood seat

1344 Billiard Chair

Same as 944 with
leather uphol-
stered or flag seat

952 Arm Chair

Height, 37½ in.
Width, 20¾ in.
Wood seat

Pool, Billiard or Combination Tables.   Standard Sizes

950

572

952

942

940

942 Arm Chair
Height, 37½ in.
Width, 21¾ in.
Wood seat

1342, the same with
leather upholstered
or flag seat

940 Chair
Height, 35¾ in.
Width, 17¾ in.
Wood seat

1340, the same with
leather upholstered
or flag seat

584 Lunch Table
Height, 30 in.
Top, 28 x 42 in.

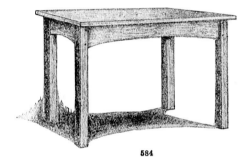

584

518 Table Desk
Height, 30 in.
Top, 24 x 36 in.

605 Double Desk
Height, 40 in.
Top, 36 x 45 in.

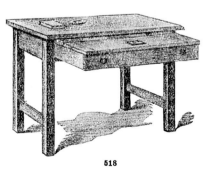

518

605